In Loving Memory Of Margaret

The Mother Tongue

H.R. Percy

Pottersfield Press
Lawrencetown Beach, Nova Scotia
1992

© H.R. Percy 1992

All rights reserved. No part of this publication may be reproduced or transmitted in any form or by any means, electronic or mechanical, or by any information storage or retrieval system, without permission in writing from the publisher.

Canadian Cataloguing in Publication Data

Percy, H.R. (Herbert Roland), 1920 -

The Mother Tongue

ISBN 0-919001-72-6

I. Title.

PS8581.E64M67 1992   C814'.54   C92-098508-4

PR9199.3.P47M67 1992

Cover art work by Geoff Butler

Published with the assistance of the Nova Scotia Department of Tourism and Culture and The Canada Council

Pottersfield Press
R.R.#2
Porters Lake
N.S. B0J 2S0 Canada

Printed and bound in Canada

CONTENTS

Introduction 5

1. THE SEASONS 9

Raspberry Fool 10
Making Hay 13
A Christmas Reverie 16
Riches of Time 20
Sweet Days and Roses 23
A Nice Book for Christmas 26
Autumn Thoughts in Ottawa 29
Two Realities 32

2. YOUTH 35

Or What's a Heaven For? 36
A Budding Poet 39
Memory and the Growing Mind 42
The Youth Cult 46

3. ART AND ATTITUDES 49

Beauty and Utility 50
Literature and the Law 53
Prudery and the Pen 57
The Illusion of Progress 60
Taste to Order 63
Quiller on the Couch 66
Fiction and History 69
Art and Individuality 73
Ill-Literacy 76
Poets' Pessimism 79
Poetic Injustice 83

The Privilege of Ignorance 86
The Age of Impatience 89
Flowers and Evil 92
Society and Solitude 95
Tolerance 98
History and Literature 101

4. THE TURNING OF LEAVES 105

Mighty Works 106
The Turning of Leaves 109
The Alice Phenomenon 112
Fact and Fiction 115
Satisfactions of The Pen 118
Books on the Shelf? 121
The Screening Process 124

5. THE MOTHER TONGUE 127

The Ize Age 128
In Defence of Adjectives 132
Philosophy and Style 136
Quotation: Its Use and Abuse 139
State of the Art 143
Simplicity and Precision 146
Experience and Expression 149
The Birth of Words 152

Introduction

Novels, short stories, essays, plays all have their beginnings somewhere back in time. Trees and plants have roots, and so do writers. Bill Percy, the author of these essays, can be followed in reverse some years before the last Great War. As a small boy of two-and-a-half years old, he was operated on for 'tubercular glands' in his neck at a hospital in Maidstone, England. He was 'delicate' for the first few years of his life, didn't join other kids at their games, became something of a 'loner' for those early years.

At home in the country, thick bushes grew at the bottom of the Percy back yard, with tunnels snaking out in all directions through the greenery. The future writer found these to be an ideal hideout and reading room, the filtered green light providing privacy for digesting literary masterpieces, like *The Magnet*, immortal heroic adventures in *Hotspur*, *Wizard*, *Gem* and other boys' weeklies of that era. Our writer hero himself was then ten, twelve, and reaching upward towards young manhood; no longer a loner and literary recluse, health more or less normal (although I wouldn't say that normality extends to all sides of his character), but still addicted to reading after being, at eight, deprived of Dickens' *Bleak House* by his mother as "too old for you." He published his own magazine at age 14, reproduced by the slow and messy 'hectograph' process, its circulation limited to Bill's family only.

I read those 'penny dreadfuls' myself when I was the same age as Bill, and their deleterious effect on my own character has been noticeable to close observers. Some of their fiction was 'school stories' and had to do with younger kids forced to be servants to older kids in senior classes. At Albert College in Belleville, Ontario, a slightly older youngster named Godspeed introduced me into that system; I was Godspeed's servant for one school semester. All as a result of Bill Percy's penny dreadfuls, whose social consequences had spread to the colonies.

George Orwell wrote an essay on these boys' weeklies in 1939, somewhat later than the time when Bill and I were feasting on them. It's a very good essay, in which the stories were described as snobbish, derivative and entirely devoid of sex. And here I must say that Bill Percy is neither snobbish nor derivative, nor is he entirely devoid of sex. (Reasons for these opinions supplied on request).

We now telescope this mini-biography somewhat. Bill Percy joined the Royal Navy in 1936 at age 16, having graduated from *Gem, Hotspur* and *Wizard*. As an engineering apprentice, he survived long and rigorous training schedules, and eventually reached the rank of Chief Engine Room Artificer. And married, in 1942, Mary Davina James, known by all as "Vina", now Bill's most devoted and vociferous publicist. And bang-bang-bang had three kids, acquired the usual worries and distractions, and did his job — in much the same way I did, although probably better.

During that long stint in the Royal Navy, Bill was writing and, latterly, publishing his stories in magazines, his writing often composed laboriously in longhand, sitting on his toolbox in the engineers' workshop while his mates were on deck sunbathing. He dreamed himself into words, becoming whatever he imagined he was, then returning to the reality of fire and grease, convoys, depth charges and war.

For the record, it should be mentioned that ERA Percy took part in the Bismarck sinking and in the Normandy invasion. Earlier, "I was supposed to join HMS *Enterprise* in Gibraltar, but the troopship I was taking passage in was attacked en route. It sank, and I floated around most of the night in the middle of the Atlantic. I had a copy of one of the novels from John Galsworthy's *Forsyte Saga* in my pocket. I lost all my own writing when the ship sank — a fact which I do not regret — but I still have that sea-stained Galsworthy.

After Bill transferred to the Canadian Navy in 1952, a rapid series of promotions followed, culminating in the rank of lieutenant commander. (This would about parallel my own rapid series of demotions in the RCAF, which caused a permanent crick in the neck from gazing upward at higher ranks). When I met Bill in the early 1960s he had already published his short stories, *The Timeless Island*, with Ryerson Press. And a novel, *Flotsam*, came a little later. Then another novel, *Painted Ladies*. Bill now claims he modeled the leading character in that last novel, Emile Logan, on me, Al Purdy. I've read the novel, and Logan doesn't resemble me in the slightest. I can't fathom what Bill Percy was thinking of when he committed this gross distortion of truth (it's a pretty good novel, though). I haven't yet decided whether to sue or schedule an appearance in small claims court. I'm now examining the later novels closely, in case Bill has D. H. Lawrence's habit of sweeping all his friends into novels as characters.

After navy discharge in 1971 Bill and Vina operated a bed and breakfast place in Granville Ferry, Nova Scotia, called The Moorings. My wife and I have visited them there several times. A few years ago my own visit coincided with that of a guest from England. He was a very old man, an ancient right out of a Thomas Hardy novel, and at the breakfast table kept touching his forelock to Bill.*

Now, placing two and two into minus 64 plus eight, I remember that penny dreadful Bill and I used to read, *Hotspur*. Now Hotspur was also the name of a scion of the aristocratic Percy family in England. Henry 'Hotspur' Percy fought at the battle of Thingamajig when knighthood was a flowering thistle. Do you suppose Bill was born on the wrong side of the bedspread and might be...? Well, I'll have to ask Vina about that.

Anyway, most of these essays were written for the Ottawa *Journal* before Bill Percy became a common civilian — even if also descended from Hotspur. The essays are rather amazing in their variety of subject matter and command of language. At the time of publication they evoked considerable comment and praise from readers; even the normally taciturn Vina has been known to mention them. I refrain, therefore, from further comment myself — except to say that Bill Percy is one of the best writers I know, unsnobbish, underivative and undevoid of sex.

I suppose that what a man is, or a woman, is largely what they've done with their lives. Many aspects of existence contribute and join to become one special thing, the culmination, if you like, being a writer in this case. I've been through the apprenticeship myself, and I'm still one. I will always be an apprentice, which is a prideful thing to be. Just as Bill Percy was an apprentice and graduated to lieutenant commander on navy discharge. More importantly, he too is a veteran apprentice writer, and I know that is a prideful thing to be for him as well.

Al Purdy
Ameliasburgh, Ontario
September, 1991.

*Pardonable poetic license. The old gentleman in question was my 'Uncle' Mick Edwards, husband of an adopted daughter of my maternal grandmother. (*H.R. Percy*)

1

The Seasons

Raspberry Fool

Wisdom waits in strange places, lowly places, places where the proud and the mighty are seldom seen and where modern man in his prison of progress is privileged to escape to less and less often. Like my raspberry patch.

It is not one of your neat, regimented raspberry patches with the canes drawn up in drill order so that you can walk sedately along the ranks like visiting royalty. It is tangled, disorderly, prolific, putting forth much new growth that can never come to anything; and not without competition from a variety of rank weeds. It reminds me of my life.

Even in this half-frivolous comparison there is food for thought. All lives are jungles, but mine more than most. I would not have it otherwise. I've had my days of discipline and conformity and I suppose that on some sterile plane of conviction they were good for my soul. I was more productive, for example, but I was productive on someone else's terms. And for someone else's profit. I was cultivated and constrained to fit the neat garden patch of society. A variety of gardeners who knew what was good for me cut off my tenderest shoots and trained my maturing growth into the way of their own narrow truths. Only late in life did I know enough to resist, to rebel, to put forth shoots in frowned-upon places and let flourish here and there a weed or two of heresy, so that my life, like my raspberry patch, became a place of discovery and mild adventure.

Going out this morning for the first time with a saucepan smaller than my hopes but bigger than my expectations, I quickly learned — and am still pondering — the lessons raspberries have to teach. As, for example, that one must tread softly and circumspectly not to crush the best of what one goes forth in search of. For the best fruits are close to the earth. They do not advertise themselves, but must be sought after with patience and understanding. They do not swell and ripen best in the full light of the sun, open to the eye of man, but deep within the shade of their own leaves, fulfilling without fanfare their own quiet purpose, which in truth is no purpose at all but a necessity of their nature.

One must lift the canes gently, not to cut off by careless handling the source of tomorrow's supply. Some are barren, some unready, but to lift up a laden stem and find it drooping under the weight of its ripe plenty is a joy of discovery that never palls. It explodes the modern fallacy that only for the first time is an experience propitious, becoming thereafter a drudgery and a source of boredom. In fact I find myself inclining more and more to the belief that what is not worth doing again and again is scarce worth doing at all.

The berries must be coaxed off with gentle fingers, used with a tenderness akin to love. And one must not aspire to reap tomorrow's harvest today, or to take by force this morning what would be freely given this afternoon; for what is taken before its time or against its inclination is bitter upon the tongue and rebellious in the belly. For the same reason one should eschew diseased or damaged fruit: an edict easier to follow for those that pick for themselves than for those that pick for profit. Your profit-seeker is not susceptible to the bellyaches of others.

One must not be averse, either, to stooping low. There are things the lofty cannot see. The richest rewards lie often sequestered, accessible only to those whose heads and hearts are close to the earth. There they cluster coy as Muses, and the unbending pass them by. I found I must not disdain to look even where there seemed to be only weeds, where often the trailing canes rested their top-heavy heads and hid their treasures among the lowlier life that grows neglected and despised. In unsuspected places, too. Disguising themselves, for example, as red currants to escape the inattentive eye (the currants being no more regimented than themselves). There are those also that trespass through the neighbour's fence; always the biggest and the best, it seems from my side. This is an outgrowth not to be reclaimed or begrudged, but to be seen rather as a source of joy at the spillover of my own plenty.

Being careful not to lose, in one's eagerness, what one has reaped already, one needs to cover the ground slowly and with thoroughness. Yet still there will be many choice berries that are missed, that will admonish me tomorrow like missed opportunities as they lie rotting on the ground. One must return again and again, finding new treasures today where there was disappointment yesterday, and desist only when the season is done.

It helps, it uplifts to pause occasionally and to ponder the mystery and the miracle of it all.

Well, when the day's picking was not quite done the sky darkened with the threat of imminent rain, reminding me how few of the things we begin in life can ever be completed. So I went indoors with my harvest, reflecting that one important part of wisdom is knowing when to quit.

Making Hay

There are few more satisfying sensations than those attending the use of a scythe: the sound of its swish and its crisp bite; the sight of the tall grass falling orderly and straight, falling as it were nobly and with honour — how different from the random impersonal reaping, the ravenous swallowing up and spewing out of a reaping machine! — and above all the rhythm and sense of rightness in our muscles that is somehow inseparable from the sound, is like the sound made feeling.

It is something between us and the grass, personal and joyful; something right, inevitable, the working out of a force of nature. It moves us to philosophic vein. But no, nothing so weighty. The thoughts float across our mind as light and wayward as the seeds of dandelions that have come overnight to white-haired age and now ascend at their call like the souls of the peaceful, submissive to a breeze that even the bonfire smoke does not suspect.

The scythe is a noble implement, perfectly adapted to the frame and motions of a man. It complements him perfectly, making with him a partnership for a just and not inordinate purpose, as does a horse or a canoe paddle. It is just sufficient to his need, not moving him to arrogance with intemperate power, not a monster he controls with trifling and unmeasured effort but an extension of himself. It responds to his muscles' precise recognition of the force required, his blood's recognition of the muscles' demands, and his breath's quickening to the call of the blood. It matches itself with him to the job at hand. It demands no fuel. It does not pollute the sweet air. It requires maintenance at no hand but its master's, and that but the touch of a stone bestowed with the gentle and practised ritual of a caress.

A noble implement indeed. Small wonder it has become symbolic. How intolerable the thought of Father Time astride a combine harvester! But is that not perhaps a symbol more appropriate to our nuclear nightmare?

It is a strange and sobering reflection, that those primeval activities by which unnumbered generations of men have won their sustenance from the soil are still, in the midst of our machine-made plenty, the most physically satisfying and the most grateful to the mind.

It is ironical to consider that man, whose unceasing aim is to save himself effort while working, must turn for relaxation to the very physical activities he has so exercised his ingenuity to escape. More ironical still, that having over the centuries devoted most of his energy and resource to escape the tyranny of the need to hunt and fish for his food, he is now prepared to pay, and pay handsomely, for the privilege if doing as a pleasure what he despised as a chore; that he will devote whole days to catching a string of fish that would have got him thrown out of the cave by any palaeolithic housewife.

It is perhaps significant also that it is the primeval implements that satisfy our need of symbol. It is the sword, not the cannon or the tank, that symbolizes war; the shield rather than the deep shelter that symbolically protects us. It is the arrow that signifies directness; the plough, fertility; the hammer, power; the scythe, symbolic reaping; the whip, tyranny. And I would suggest that these maintain supremacy not merely because they were first in the field. After all, we change everything else in response to the demands of an illusory progress, why not our symbols? Is it not perhaps that these things owe their symbolism to the fact that they demand an effort commensurate with the result? Is it not perhaps that our modern, something-for-nothing philosophy is incapable of creating meaningful symbols?

A recent magazine article depicted and deplored the age-long use of man as a beast of burden. One could only share the writer's horror at this degradation but it is important to remember that the degradation lay not in the carrying of the burden, but in the fact that it was another's burden; that one man should be exploited, degraded to the level of a beast in order that another might reap the rewards in luxury and idleness.

Inevitable, in the implied comparison of this past — but by no means yet entirely past — slavery with the dawning of this automated Utopia, there was a suggestion that toil is ignoble, unworthy of modern man. This seems indeed to be the infirm rock upon which our philosophy of progress is founded. All that is really ignoble is the use of a man as a beast. Or as a machine.

Toil is not ignoble, and our blood and sinews know it. The man who harnesses all week long at the press of a button the power of a stampeding buffalo herd is never more truly attuned to himself than when, at the week's end, he submits himself to the simple, ancient life-rituals of carrying water, cutting wood, digging the soil or cutting back with joyful scythe the brush that presses in upon the small space he occupies at Nature's sufferance.

A Christmas Reverie

The propensity of overfed adults to sleep away whole glorious Christmas afternoons was always a source of surprise and vexation to me. How could they, at the very meridian of the day's excitement, simply run down like the clockwork toys my puny fingers had not the strength to rewind? Many a vow I made that when I came to man's broad-waistcoated estate, to the dignity of watch-chain and whiskers, I would never be guilty of such dereliction.

The years have made me more sympathetic to those departed forty-winkers: uncles clutching the slow fuses of their cigars that always disappointingly went out before the uncles were detonated into wakefulness; aunts whose emancipated top teeth cannibalized their lower lips while their knitting needles languished in mid-stitch; Grandfather, who never woke up when I pried his fingers from the book he had been reading to me, but merely sank his head a little lower so that his white beard fanned out to confer, absurdly, a saintliness upon him as he mumbled sailor's profanities under his moustache; and Grandmother, her spectacles continuing to read the Good Book long after her eyes had succumbed, her very snores ascending like prayers.

The observance of most vows becomes easier with habit, but this one I must confess is an exception. Each year it has proved a little more difficult to sustain enthusasm for toy trains, or to read with unflagging gusto to the youngsters while the angel of sleep hovers close. Increasingly, I become aware that I misjudged those gentle snoozers of the past. They had their own vision of bliss, such as no mere toy-beguiled or bookworm infant can appreciate. The seductions of sleep are great. Replete and savouring still the vintage port, they drifted into it as easily and blissfully as I was borne into the enchanted world of *The Wind in the Willows* or *Treasure Island*.

I have always kept the vow, however, and as I sit here wreathed in cigar-smoke, watching the child at play, my will is strong. Sooner or later he will want something wound up, or will have a sudden desire to be read to, and I must not fail. How well I recall the urgency of the need to know the secrets locked in the black regiments of print, and the frustration of finding no one awake to supply the key.

In the newspaper I notice an advertisement for Christmas stockings for dogs. What nonsense, I begin to say, but all the others are asleep. My own dog, stockingless but gorged from the plates of children with eyes bigger than bellies, snores shamelessly on the rug. I begin to feel a little superior in my wakefulness.

My armchair enfolds me, shaping itself to my need like an embrace. I sink deep into thought about the folly of pampering animals. As if it makes any difference to them whether it's Christmas or not. As if they care about their goodies being in a stocking. What fools we humans be.

"Agreed on the last count, but as for the rest, aren't you being a little smug?"

I could swear there was a voice, but a fire-truck collides with my foot, shattering my reverie. Rover's eyelids drift down, veiling a strange gleam. Turning the page, I read about books; resolve to read them, but know there will never be time. On the page opposite, a reindeer extols the merits of somebody's bread. Its grammar is not good.

Buried among the want-ads there is a small news item stating that an American university is conducting an experiment with a chimpanzee. The animal is to be brought up in every respect as a human child, beginning immediately with diapers and formula and progressing from there. I reflect that there may be some difficulty with the school board, or at least with the home and school. My neighbour Birtwhistle has a monkey, so I know what folly all this is. He brings it when he comes to visit. It never strikes me as being particularly intelligent. We're a little too glib with our talk about being almost human. It has some clever tricks, of course, but...

The child climbs on my lap.

"Let's read, eh? You promised."

My paper floats to the floor. We open *Toad of Toad Hall* and I begin to read. He listens enthralled, but glancing up after a while I observe that his eyes seem to be getting heavy. A little devil whispers in my ear, "If you let him fall asleep first..." I thrust the devil aside. "Here," I say to the child. "Show me how well you can read."

He comes out of his trance and looks at me accusingly.

"Or perhaps the book's too hard for you?"

He frowns, but takes the book and reads, hesitating a little over the longer words. I listen to Toad extolling motor cars and the joys of the open road. A born mimic, that boy. I listen to the dialogue. The accents of childhood so perfectly complement it that the characters are as vividly alive for me as when I read the book for the first time, many, many years ago.

"You shouldn't carry on so," says Water Rat. "You'll be getting us animals a bad name."

"Our name stinks anyway," Toad replies. "We're just second-class citizens."

"Wait," I put in. "I don't remember that part."

Toad looks at me scornfully. Rover stands up slowly, stretches and comes over.

"He's right. It's time we stood up for ourselves. All this animal prejudice has got to stop. We're all animals under the skin."

"Yes," fumed Toad, puffing up with indignation. "Just because we're a little different outside you think you can patronize us and persecute us. Well, you can't."

"He's right, by St. George," Rover says.

"St. George?"

"Orwell."

"Oh."

"If we had equal opportunities we'd be as good as you."

"Better," says Rover. He goes and gets my jacket and cap from the hall and puts them on. "See? It's only clothes that make the man. Give us education and equal rights and in no time we'll have a class-free society."

"Give us the vote."

"And Christmas stockings," adds Water Rat wistfully.

"Nonsense. That's for pups." Rover is getting nasty. He bares his teeth and shakes his paw in my face. He begins to shout. A door slams, and new voices join the commotion. The animals, in ugly mood, press in upon me. One of them seizes me by the nose. The others laugh uproariously.

I close my eyes upon the frightening scene. The child it seems has stopped reading and is bouncing up and down on my knees, making a strange chattering noise. When I open my eyes again a moment later I find the child's chimpanzee-like face thrust close to mine. His fingers are entwined in my beard.

"Stop it," I say sternly, "and get on with the story."

Rover, dressed up in my coat and hat, sits regarding me mournfully, his head on one side. The older child, just back from skating, lies convulsed with laughter on the floor.

Birtwhistle stands there grinning like a fool.

"Merry Christmas all," he says.

The others wake up, startled. I'm glad I wasn't caught napping.

Riches of Time

The year is still to all intents new, merely nibbled at. We have it excitingly in our hands like a pay cheque cashed but not spent. It gives us a heady sense of wealth; of resources at hand for endeavours of our own choosing, for the fulfilment of our own glowing vision. Bright of eye and prodigal of purpose, we think of the deeds that might be done — that have been done — by the energies at one man's call.

In this exalted state, telling our riches of time, we are prone to resolutions. We will read enormously: the Himalayas of books we simply must read, towering yearly more formidable upon the cloudy horizon of our conscience, are revealed to be after all accessible to determined attack. We will cultivate anew our legion of neglected friends, write prodigiously to those absent, visit and entertain those who, separated from us by the far-flung continents of private preoccupation, live on the next street. We will restore our languishing virtues and throw off the tyranny of our vices: or perhaps vice versa, if dull habit has made conformity irksome. These Goliaths and a dozen such we confront with the puny sling of our resolve. The year's youth seems ours: all things are possible.

We refuse as yet to recognize that these riches are largely committed, that we have sunk into debt with society. When our tithe of daily work is exacted, concession made to the cries of the flesh, and tribute of time rendered to family and friends, what small sediment of vitality will remain for the pursuit of stars? Of all this untapped wealth, how small the change that will rattle at last in the capacious pocket of our free will?

We speak often of saving time. If only we could. How convenient if we could hoard like misers the golden minutes that slip away because they are too small to do great things with. It is as if we threw away the change from every dollar because it will not buy us a new house, and so squandered half our income. There is not time to further this or that grand scheme before supper, we tell ourselves (supper being by inference more important than all our endeavours), and so we do nothing. Or there are not enough minutes before bedtime to open *War and Peace*, that has lain upon the shelf these five years in mute accusation. As if we fancied that some time there will be a week in which to do nothing but read War and Peace. But there is time before bed to turn on the television, and if our interest is won, or our inertia great, we find after all that bedtime is elastic.

Many are the people I have met who say, with that faraway look of a poet in labour, that they really must write something one day — when they have time. Or they really must try their hand at painting a picture, or must study music, or move a mountain. It is a hard lesson to learn, that great deeds are done by the minute, the mountains of ambition moved a shovelful at a time. The mountains tower immense, and the shovel is a puny implement; but it serves well enough for us to lean upon while we dream of bulldozers and backhoes and dynamite. It is not easy, in the awful shadow of the peaks, to retain our New Year clarity of vision, our resolute glow. It is difficult to persuade ourselves, when the goal is obscured by obstacles, that, were it easy to do, it would not be worth the doing, that only the obstacles make it a goal at all. However little "free time" we have, the regular application of that little to a steady purpose can achieve marvels.

Others see the problem in a different light. Theirs is a lack not of time but of direction. They have plenty of time but no purpose: bulldozers and dynamite but no mountains. Their lives, they lament, are dull, their circumstances not fruitful of remarkable achievement. Living in a drab, dispiriting suburbia, working a monotonous round at an obscure job, they feel themselves imprisoned by the ordinary, cocooned in the commonplace. "What hope have I of making a mark in the world," Smith says. "I am only a teacher." Or, "I am only a private in the army." To which one can only reply, "So was Socrates. So was Napoleon. Their circumstances were no more propitious than yours." Their greatness after all consisted in the extent and excellence of their achievement, rather than in the nature of what they achieved.

We have only to consider the great variety of fields in which men have distinguished themselves to see the truth of this. The most exalted of pursuits could be made to look ridiculous and futile if viewed with complete objectivity, in isolation from the totality of achievement that has shed glory upon them; Columbus sailing the endless ocean, Hans Andersen scribbling fairy tales, the Wrights playing with their flying contraptions: were they not fools? The painters of pictures and the writers of poems are frivolous shirkers of social responsibility, until they have somehow by their complete dedication and the totality of their achievement conferred nobility upon their enterprise.

We can only justify any pursuit by the degree of our faith in it, by the extent to which we give ourselves to it. One cannot be a passive saint. Life has no meaning apart from our own endeavours. We can make any work noble by giving the whole of ourselves to it: not our labour only, but our imagination, our integrity, our love.

Perhaps after all we should do well to celebrate our New Years by doing nothing, while we meditate a little upon who we are, and where we are going, and what it is we ask of life.

Then let us to our shovels.

Sweet Days and Roses

We might say perhaps with Coleridge: "...the spring comes slowly up this way."
Winter seems to play out his stern repertoire before spring is ready for her cue. There are days when looking down at the drab sandy sidewalks and the gutters with their sooty lingerings of snow, the very earth seems inert, enduring but without promise, like an old oak stump. But if in the midst of all our care and tension — that malady unknown to the ancients, whose lives were more precarious yet than ours — we suffer our glance to stray aloft, we surprise the sky vernal and exalting among the naked treetops; a brief glimpse only, before the clouds flock back one last time to confound the premature takers-off of snow tires and to flutter the breast of skiers with extravagant expectancy, soon dashed. In these days the frigid purity of winter is tarnished — become meaningless like that of a sere spinster — and the purity of renewal and growth has not yet come. But there is everywhere such a gurgling and a stirring in sleep, such a throwing off of icy thralldom where not long since the children skated and snowballed, that we hang on to our hope. There is relief in the air, as if Mother Earth had let loose her stays. Ever and again between the last petulant backward glances of Old Hoary Head we glimpse the spring, airy and remote as a politician's promise, caught in the macabre clutch of branches.
You cannot shut the windows of the sky.
And so spring, more potent and sure than our faith, at last comes on apace. We see everywhere the lithe grace of squirrels, black ripples across the roadway. Leaner than Cassius from the long winter's frugality, they run by some spaceman's magic up and down trees where no foothold is possible. They make

prodigious leaps of faith to land on twigs that would not support a fly. They streak across the power lines with a poise and agility that puts great Blondin's memory to shame.

Newcomers to the city begin to have hallucinations of rabbits.

C'est le printemps! Even our laboured bilingualism bears living fruit. We return from our first Sunday venture *à la campagne* muddy to the roof but triumphant with budding pussy willows, ourselves budding with optimism and a new bonhomie. All along the wayside we have seen trees glowing at the tips like six-week blondes, and the fallow earth shocking the eye with brown and voluptuous nakedness. On the lakes the ice darkens and shrinks prudish from the warm touch of earth; but on the shores and in the almost-secluded bowers we see, wiser, the young lovers strolling. The young men's faces suddenly aglow with life's meaning, inspired to faith and purpose by

The kiss, snatched hasty from the sidelong maid.

All around there is such a thrusting and reviving, such jubilation among all creatures, such awakening to beauty and to life. We hardly know whether the new brightness is around or within us.

And that evening in our armchairs, drunk with spring air, we read that Nature is out of date, or perhaps even dead, like God. Wherever we turn, the story is the same. Nature must make way for the great god Progress. To science, she is but a predecessor of limited ability whose work is to be exploited and improved upon. And in the arts, nature is a dirty word. "Nature poet," and "nature painter" are terms of contempt. Poets of every generation preceding our own are lumped together under this disparaging epithet. They were, we are told, out of touch with the concerns of their time. Perhaps they were, but I begin to suspect that we are losing touch with something even more vital, not only to the flourishing of art but to the continuance of life.

A hundred years ago, men still saw Nature as the supreme artist, and creative man as but her puny imitator and extoller.

> But who can paint like nature? Can imagination boast
> Amid its gay creation, hues like hers?

They carried it, admittedly, to extremes. But so do we. Our swing of the pendulum carries us into follies more egregious than theirs, and leaves us suspended over an abyss, a frightful vacancy.

It is our great failure that we have allowed nature to become "out of date", and in spring, briefly, we know it. Among all this splendour and renewal we cannot but be aware where lies the source of all our strength, our wisdom, our hope. We have but to sniff the air of these spring mornings to know that politics are unimportant, commerce is paltry, unbridled "industry" an abomination. But still we lop off with desperate energy the hydra-heads of nature that spring forth and multiply to menace our artificial world. We seem incapable of learning Wordsworth's lesson, that

> One single impulse from a vernal wood
> May teach you more of man,
> Of moral evil and of good,
> Than all the sages can.

And we do not yet seem to have caught the terrible echo of the title of Rachel Carson's book, to have comprehended the true horror of that year when the spring will, indeed, be silent.

A Nice Book For Christmas

One of the great appeals of Christmas is that under the season's spell even the most practical of us may be shamelessly nostalgic; may sweeten the present by remembering — perhaps erroneously — how good things were in the past. It is a time when memories may be heightened a little, and idealized like snow-scenes on Christmas cards. And this is good: it restores one's faith, and one's hope, and one's charity. Although we lament the decline from an imagined ideal, we lament it with a glow in our hearts of assurance that what has once been — even if only in the imagination — may surely be again.

All this stems from tradition, a thing too little regarded in these days. Goodwill emanates from us because we find security and excitement in the recurrence of familiar things. Even the lament for better times departed has become a tradition. Part of the fun lies in vying with others in evoking the past to prove that no Christmas is ever quite equal to those preceding it. The plum puddings are never quite so large, the company never so jolly, the children never so completely enthralled. The truth is, of course, that hearts are never quite so youthful.

There is an ache in the human soul for permanence, for the comfort of the familiar and the stable. It is a yearning less and less assuaged as social and scientific changes gather momentum. There is a tendency among the so-called progressive elements in society to belittle the importance of this vital human need for reference points in the past, for a foot on the sure and solid ground of things well known, and, because well known, well loved.

It is even suggested by some that this yearning is a bad thing, a lamentable human weakness that must be vanquished if man is to attain the high promise of his materialistic civilization. The human race cannot completely fulfill itself while its individual members concern themselves with the perpetuation of outworn institutions (outworn in this case meaning not recently changed); while they stubbornly persist in calling one place home, one habitual way their own, and while they dream upon the past. While he is bound by his heartstrings to the past, goes the argument, man can only bend reluctantly to the forces of progress. He cannot float free and completely adaptable upon the currents of change. He will always be to some extent static so long as he has roots. It is perhaps futile to ask by what means he will be nourished when at last he has none.

But even the most dour disclaimers of man's right to lead his life, rather than to be led by it, tend to relent at Christmastime, to become mellow, put aside their poses and sing Auld Lang Syne. Perhaps even they will forgive me if I pause to dream of those old-time crowded Christmases when there was somehow time for an hour or two with a good book. And when somehow there always was a good book. If there were fewer books in those days, at least there were also fewer bad books.

There were good books, and people knew how to give them. One of the hard facts of a writer's life is that everyone gives him books for Christmas. He becomes one of the easy-to-please, one whose gift requires no thought, like one of those distant nephews and nieces who receive a postal order every year. He is sent a "nice book" ("nice" being applied to books in the same vague sense, unrelated to quality, in which a Cockney speaks of "a nice cup o' tea") and his complete satisfaction is taken for granted. Very few people seem to be aware that the giving of books is a difficult undertaking, requiring intimate knowledge and a decided flair. Choosing a book for a man can be almost as great a presumption as choosing him a wife. Certainly there are fewer successful book givers in the world than successful matchmakers. Or, for that matter, successful writers.

It was not always so. There has been a sad decline in the art. Or is it simply that over the years we have become more difficult to please? It seems to me that the aunts and uncles of the past had a keener appreciation of the literary tastes of nieces and nephews than those of today. It is true that their choice was easier. The range was narrower, and the chances were that they had themselves read the books they gave. They were naive enough to believe that their own past enjoyment was a reliable criterion of selection. Any modern child knows what nonsense this is. No book that has been read by an uncle or aunt can possibly be any good.

There was also a quaint idea abroad that books, like wine, were matured and proved by time, that the more generations of readers a book had delighted, the safer it was to give. Today, of course, we know that absolute novelty is the only test of a book's worth and the key to successful book-giving. Books must be bought piping hot like muffins. To offer a book published three months ago is like serving yesterday's oatmeal for breakfast.

Another remarkable thing about those aunts and uncles was that they had the temerity to choose books for children without any guidance from psychologists, school teachers, librarians and others who know so much more than mere book-lovers how to choose a book. They recklessly made their own choice, and somehow they were uncannily right: although right only in the sense that their gifts delighted those that received them. No doubt today's experts could prove them hopelessly wrong.

Of course there were always means of apprising parents and others of one's outlandish literary preferences; ways so devious and subtle that the dear simple folk were obviously deceived by one's affectation of surprise when the coveted book came forth from its wrapper. And such is the power of make-believe that their pleasure in seeing one surprised induced surprise itself, and the true delight drove out the counterfeit. They in turn were delighted at their perceptiveness in making the right selection, all on their own.

In those days it was books that saved the occasion from dread anticlimax when more fleeting pleasures palled. In those later doldrums of the day when surfeited elders slept and the young were enjoined to silence, then could one sprawl amid the ribbons and wrappings and nutshells at the feet of Grandmother snoozing surreptitiously over her Bible, open the shiny covers and enter one's own world.

Autumn Thoughts in Ottawa

Autumn, season of admonition, time of paradox! Along the Rideau Canal already trees are shedding their less tenacious illusions. In these first chill mornings the mists rise but a foot or two from the water and soon vanish, their intimations of mortality only for the early abroad. Squirrels go about their business like Christmas Eve shoppers. Everywhere soon there will be gold, not for gathering; everywhere beauty, poignant, crying its own impermanence. Old Omar sings with diminishing conviction in the wilderness.

There is a vicariousness in our delight, as if the present were already a memory. Even in the balmiest noons an airy foot walks over the grave of the waters, and we feel with them in anticipation the relentless clutch of ice. The warmth and brilliance become but yardsticks of the cold to come. Our sweetest enjoyments acquire an edge. The evening smell of woodsmoke is acrid with nostalgia. The trivial accustomed sounds of summer ring hollow with farewell. Every sunset is a valediction.

No less than in spring we are restless, but it is no longer the restlessness of high adventure, of wide horizons; it is the unease of things not done and the running out of sands; of talents committed neither wisely nor well. Even the young feel fleetingly the brush of years, and their exigency; are touched with urgency and determination to eke the last out of life. Their play seems more purposeful, more intense, as if they are precociously aware the moving finger writes, even upon the wall where they perform their innocent, ball-bouncing miracles.

Early frost is the year's first warning, rheumatic twinge. It gives a man pause to digest the hard lesson of his waning prime. Henceforth it will not be roses all the way. Procrastination exacts its price. The things we put off yesterday demand a little more effort today. It will cost us pain to do them tomorrow. In the days to come, though we see so much more clearly the need, we may be powerless to do them at all, at any price.

The trees are mirrors to our mixed emotions. The willows are Magdalenes mourning. The maples blush rebellious to the roots of their red hair, resigned to die like heretics. The poplars stand proud in line, waiting their turn, but their aspen sisters twitter and shake with spinsterly fears. Dark in priestlike garb, the spruces wait Pharisee-smug for the fires to die; inquisitors, aloof, unbending, assured of salvation. Only the mountain ash, loaded with riches, garish as a harlot, swaggers and laughs defiance, living it up. Naked like the rest but decked out with her jewellery still, she will laugh a little ruefully and say to the March wind: "See, so you can take it with you!"

Yet with it all, what exhilaration! With the morning air sharp in our nostrils we stride exultant. All our sensibilities are whetted to a keen edge. Beauty takes us by the throat, rubs our noses in the ugliness that we have made, leaves us chastened and full of aspiration; late, but doubly urgent for that. It is the year's second season of resolutions. How much wiser the Jews, to have their New Year now: for how different things look from this, the sober side of the year. When the carefree time is all before us to lavish and squander, that is no time to be making resolutions. But when we see the squirrels laying up for themselves treasures in their snug, secret heavens, what an example they offer to the pious and impious alike!

In January, with spring's plenty not yet broached and all the summer days yet to come, we could afford to defer the labour that would unlock our dreams. But now, when all about us is fruitful and life is brimming over with bounty, suddenly the leaves begin to drift down and our remaining moments with them. We measure our dreams against the days that fly. When very young we pointed peashooters at the stars, and from where we stood the try fell not, it seemed, so very far short.

It is a time of doing, of gathering and garnering. Too late for lamenting what was never sown, or not cultivated with enough care. We in the city are largely spared the old urgency to be up and doing against the coming of winter, the recurring object-lesson of the seasons that keeps the countryman in touch with truth. But we cannot altogether evade the sober reflections of the fall, nor altogether avoid that seasonal shift in our perspective which, if we will pay heed, will make us wiser and better. For being surrounded by so much beauty, and finding around us reminders that its time and ours will be so short, it is less easy to be petty in our thought; less easy to bow to our greed instead of our good conscience, less easy to hate than to love. Our reading, like our thought, takes a more sober and weighty turn. Literary good intentions bear a little fruit. We find ourselves scanning wistfully the shelves where repose those many volumes purchased at ambition's impulse, against a more leisured time. We reflect perhaps a little sadly that the road to hell is paved with unread books. They confront us, those unkept promises to ourselves, and we become aware that the space each fills corresponds to an emptiness within: our mind had prepared a place against their coming. Vague yearning sharpens into hunger.

Patient in a shadowed corner of my own shelves wait many unmade and long-neglected friends: Marcus Aurelius, Burton, Thomas à Kempis, Whitman, Stevenson, Flaubert... I contemplate them for a long, sad-sweet time, and come away carrying Goethe's Faust. That's what started all this.

Two Realities

The sky today is magnificent. I have watched it for many minutes, pondering its mystery. I have plucked my subject, literally, out of the clouds. They are wispy and white, imperceptibly multiplying and assuming substance as the day advances. No discernible movement, yet while I lose myself for a minute or two in reverie they change in shape and complexion. They are transformed completely yet retain some subtle vestige of identity, as do we humans with the years. They join, divide, alter continually their posture one to another. The west pours a golden warmth upon my complacency but the east has an aspect of storm.

There is a great deal of philosophy to be had for nothing out of the sky. It is hard to believe that it is all a lie; barely possible to persuade ourselves it does not exist. We know very well there is nothing but endless vacancy; a layer of gases, invisible but by their depth creating, like tropic waters, a blue illusion; and a few wisps of water vapour made sport of as the gases stir in endless convection. No more.

Yet the mind puts something there. The mind will have something there whether our knowledge sanctions it or not. From this immensity of nothing and these few insubstantials our senses fashion a unified tangible something that can be embraced in a single word — sky. It is not an abstract concept, such as we express by the word "space." It is something we can see. And when it is not visible we can imagine it, without effort.

We can paint it (although not without effort). We can make a symbol of it for all that is ultimate, all that is exalted, and people it with gods. It is a dome that will comfortably contain the limits of our comprehension, a roof under which we can shelter from our perplexities and doubts, from all the questions our curiosity has started from the complex and awful Pandora's box of the universe. It provides us with a defence, in the form of a reality we can live with, against the reality we can not.

Of all the things the sky symbolizes, it provides above all an analogy for the duality that has plagued man ever since he framed his first question about the world in which he found himself. Ever since, that is to say, he ceased to be an animal and became a man; for it is this appetite for the why and wherefore of things that man alone has additional to all other appetites and propensities found in living creatures. It is his glory and his curse.

It is his curse because it has revealed to him two realities: that which his senses present to him, and within which he must live; and that which investigation and inference have assured him is there. The first is the reality that encompasses a sky where the second offers mist and emptiness. One is composed of substances and objects and people while the other is a vast random orgy of electronic commotion, fascinating and rather fearful in its complexity but meaningless within the narrow compass of the human mind.

We tend to distinguish between appearance and reality, but we have in truth no way of determining what reality is. If we accept the reality perceptible to our senses, life becomes simple and seems to have meaning; but the reality deducible through our intellect makes it necessary for us to live a lie. The very self becomes a delusion begotten of a world of shadows. But for a negative charge or two my flesh would be wood, my blood water, my breath fire. How is one to retain sanity and direction in a world where the only reality is the beehive hum of energy, the only distinction, between negative and positive?

It is this profound schism in our philosophy of life, this rent in the foundation of our faith, that is the basis of the great "two cultures" controversy, the war between humanity and science that can never be resolved. At best there can be a truce, with man making the best of both worlds: accepting the evidence of his senses and reaping the riches of his environment while interpreting and profiting by his scientific discoveries as if they were dreams. He can live a normal and satisfying life only to the extent that he subscribes to the grand hallucination, to the extent that he accepts the testimony of his own perception, even though he knows that testimony to be false.

The art of living thus becomes a matter of selection, of consciously or unconsciously deciding at any moment what reality one will accept and what reject; what shall be one's truth and what illusion and falsehood; what we shall see, and how we shall see it. We can believe in objects only as we see and feel them; sounds as they fall upon the ear and flavours as we relish them upon the palate, as sensations rather than as pressure-waves or squiggles on paper or chemical reactions.

Above all, we can believe in people only as we perceive them, and love them only as the entire beings our senses present to us. There are times when we must close our minds to the knowledge science has accumulated within us, and live in the world of sensual reality. There is no nourishment to be had from a plate a bacteria: much from a good steak. There is no physical or spiritual fulfillment to be achieved by embracing an apparatus of nerves, blood, bone and muscle, a complex of chemical processes or a swarm of molecular activity: much, however, if we can persuade ourselves that these constitute a man or a woman.

All becomes, it seems, a matter of faith. One must make the gesture of acceptance of the physical "realities" upon which any meaning of life must be premised. Without such a gesture there can be no answers, only questions. It is as such a gesture, such an act of faith, that art in general and literature in particular are significant and necessary, and will become increasingly so as scientific investigation of man and of the cosmos progresses.

2

Youth

Or What's a Heaven For?

Somewhere in that uncharted time before I was ten I had my first encounter with literary censorship. I remember it, as I remember many another baptismal moment of pain and mortification, with almost stereoscopic clarity. Wedged between our warm bright living kitchen and the general store that was our precarious source of income there was a small windowless room that aspired to be a parlour. In this it was thwarted on weekdays by the need to tramp through it to get to the shop, and by the presence of the telephone, which, being the only one in the village, was in considerable demand. But on Sundays when the shop was closed the gaslight made magic in the little room. The flicker of firelight on the brass fender warmed the very heart of childhood, and one neither knew nor cared that it was raining outside. It always was.

It was an atmosphere in which my love of books could not but flourish, although apart from the fact that for some obscure unliterary reason my grandfather was nicknamed "Poet" there was no precedent or particular encouragement for it. But high up there was a hanging bookcase containing a few finely bound volumes that by their very aloofness took on an air of magnificent promise, seemed to hint at a felicity comparable with that of the Kingdom of Heaven, and certainly more accessible to the imagination. Their effect upon me, in their seductive remoteness, was like that of the voluptuous leading ladies in the pantomimes we were taken to see at Christmas in the Theatre Royal in Chatham; an allure no less potent for being but dimly understood. In reading, also, I was precocious.

These books in their grandeur bore no more relation to the common books that lay about the kitchen or the grimy volumes I lugged to school than the leading ladies bore to the scrawny daughters of the drunk next door. They were celestial books, books transcending books, replete with all knowledge, all wisdom, all intimations of beauty and delight. No one ever took them down.

For years I was content to admire them with humility as I admired the stars, drawing from them a strange unquestioned comfort and a deep, mysterious sustenance. But all the time I was reading avidly, with an addict's abandon, and as my slowly increasing altitude diminished — though not by much — the gulf that lay between me and that far-off milky way of words, I began to discern titles, and to speculate. It could only be a matter of time.

BLEAK HOUSE. It was bang in the middle, magnificent in maroon leather with filigrees of gold. My fingers yearned for the feel of it. My mind fondled the words of the title as if it had been an absent beloved's name, and I wove my own fantasies about it more rich than even its fertile author dreamed of. At last I mountaineered the plush slopes of the armchair-back and took it down; really held it, heavy and momentous, in my hands. Its pages were yellow-brown at the edges, paling towards the centre where the regiments of words were drawn up for my inspection. I carried the treasure to my favourite corner and sat for a long time in dreamy anticipation.

"Boy, that's much too old for you." My mother's glasses twinkled with amusement. I had been "Boy" for years as an expedient to distinguish me from my sister, but now that I had a brother it still slipped out sometimes as an endearment. But she was very firm: not with any suggestion of bearing down any resistance I might offer, but with a grown-up's quiet air of knowing what is best. I am sure now that if I had demonstrated in some way the potency of my desire to meet the challenge of the book, my mother would have conceded, and probably after a few pages would have been in a position to say, "I told you so." But parental opinion was a powerful force. I handed over *Bleak House* without question.

She made a great mistake, my kind, well-meaning mother. She wanted to save me from struggle and disappointment, from the imagined harm of tackling something that was too much for me. But these are the very things that build the muscles of the mind, that temper the edge of taste. Now that I recall it, all my youthful reading was precocious, half-comprehending. How can one have it otherwise, and grow? Much of what I read was "beyond" me. Thus it was I learned: not only in the sense of acquiring knowledge, but by thrilling to the slowly unfolding wonder of what could be done with words. Sometimes I laboured through whole books and carried away from them nothing but an awed awareness of the potency of the words in which they were written, or a dim shape in my mind of something that belonged unmistakably to that author and no other: the shape, as I was to appreciate much later, of his style.

This is a lesson we all must learn — that educators need to learn and that the writers of children's books need to learn — that it is better to let a child choose a book and understand one-tenth of it than to choose for him a book that has been written for his "age group" so that all his faculties can sleep while he passively enjoys it. Many will be the books he starts and never finishes, but in the mere act of starting them, of embarking upon them as upon a voyage of adventure, he will feel himself immeasurably enriched: and their challenge, the promise they hold out of something deep and exciting and wonderful, will bring him back again and again insatiate, long after those that have been fed literary pablum have embraced a lifelong diet of comic books and their television equivalent.

I never did read *Bleak House*.

A Budding Poet

Forgive me, madam, if I continue our conversation in public. Your son, you were saying, wants to be a poet. After a moment the pride ebbed from your eyes to expose a lively apprehension. The others nodded sympathetically over their cocktails. Especially the one whose eldest girl recently went wrong.

"I can't imagine where he gets it from." I could tell that mentally you were going over all the skeletons on both sides of the ancestral closet.

"Probably from you."

Your eyes questioned my motives. Deciding to take it as a compliment, you blushed and protested. It was not a compliment.

"It's very difficult to know what to do."

"Don't do anything," I said.

You were still uncertain whether to show interest or indignation when your face was eclipsed by a blue serge shoulder and our host was boisterously introducing Charlie. In Charlie's presence, poetry simply was not possible.

I had been about to point out, madam, that if there is poetry in the boy, nothing you wilfully do, short of infanticide, is likely to stop it coming out, although it may well influence what comes out, and that to your very great surprise. If the environment you have created for him is making a writer of him, well-intentioned meddling on your part is more than likely to louse things up, to have an effect opposite to your intention.

Many parents find themselves in this dilemma. Their child shows an artistic bent. They feel an obligation to encourage it, but they are deficient in faith. They know neither the measure of the child's potential nor the strength of his resolve. To them, success is more important than what is succeeded at. A successful accountant is more worthy than an unsuccessful poet. They foist accountancy upon him, or dentistry upon her, thus perhaps setting in the child's way the ultimate pain that will crystalize the resolve to write, or will set in train the slow precipitation of worldly cares that will frustrate that resolve for ever.

The ultimate pain? I see your pencilled eyebrows lift a little at this. Yes, madam. Pain.

"But my Johnny has wanted for nothing. He has been sheltered from all harm. Pain, indeed."

Witness then Gabriel Fielding, a novelist of stature not so very far inferior to that of his namesake Henry: "I write out of pain — I believe most writers do."

This is the sort of statement non-writers (and writers with short memories) misunderstand and mistrust, but it is fundamentally true. The desire to write, or paint, or engage lifelong in any imaginative pursuit, arises out of an attitude to life engendered by pain; pain in the broadest, usually non-physical, sense of the word.

Most writers know very early in life that they are going to be writers, though they may be far from young when they emerge as such. Life has a habit of getting in the way. But this certitude comes into being as an imaginative antidote to some painful or oppressive experience. It is a flinching from something unpleasant in life and a seeking, instead, of the ideal; a turning inward in search of a world where such pain and oppression are not possible, or, if possible, are conquerable.

It results, usually, from books; from the escape into others' imaginings; from the recognition of emotional affinities; from the blessed balm of language. There is a time of discovery that one's pain may not be, after all, the true or the only reality. One begins to glimpse a way of escape. But not of escape only; of triumph, of vindication, of proving oneself, pre-eminently, a person of worth.

It may take little or much: a few repeated humiliations by a bully or a whole long childhood of tyranny, a thoughtless withholding of love or the soul-ravages of war. What is necessary is the arrival at a point early in life where it becomes easier to confront oneself than to confront the world; where one is forced to break through the barrier into the imagination and call for strength upon one's own introspective resources. It is a barrier that thickens and calcifies with age, becoming at last impenetrable.

In reality there is no escape, for it does not take long to discover that it is much more painful to sit and ponder upon life than to enter thoughtlessly into it. One can create worlds for others only at the expense of one's own. The poet can catch life on the wing, but he cannot live while he is doing it.

So, who can say what is prerequisite to the emergence of an artist? Encouragement of an apparent creative talent may produce only an opinionated bore; the suppression of it, a genius. It seems, madam, that the only recipe for producing a poet is to subject him alternately to all the cruelties of which we are capable, and to shut him up in a library. The same recipe, unfortunately, could produce a gangster or a politician.

It is alarming to speculate that when at last psychiatry has straightened everybody out, when all occasion for emotional disturbance in the young has been eliminated, there will be no more art. Perhaps it will be necessary to expose selected persons to creativity-engendering pain in the same way that laboratory animals are exposed, in the cause of science, to disease.

If you are optimistic, madam, about the future, encourage your son to become an accountant. In a perfect world there would be no poets.

Memory and the Growing Mind

Memory is a strange and fickle thing. Yet it is by this mysterious and unreliable instrument that we are formed; by it our characters, our destinies, our very bodies are shaped. What we remember is what we are.

This is not to suggest that the better our memories, the more worthy we are as men and women, or more noble, or more anything except perhaps more reliable to be sent for the groceries. For the process is irrational, ungovernable, and largely involuntary. The memories that affect us most deeply and linger the longest with us often steal into our consciousness unawares, sometimes even against our will. They insinuate themselves into our very blood, condition our every act and thought.

Since children become living products of the things they remember, and since parents are notoriously meddlesome in the destinies of their children, there is a natural desire to ensure that children remember the right things. This is all we are doing when we apply the teachings of child psychologists: and we all know how futile that can be. While you are trying so earnestly to impress upon little Ray the importance of eating this or that, he is probably salting down a lifelong memory of the way vexation drives a wedge of shadow between your eyes. If you urge *Treasure Island* upon him, in all probability the only thing he will remember of the book in after years will be that you made him read it.

But if we cannot consciously improve our children by regulating what their memory shall accept and what reject, we can help them so to broaden the scope of their experience, that in grazing at random over the rich pastures of literature, they will happen upon the fullest measure of what is good and true and wholesome. Unhappily, these excellent words, 'good', 'true' and 'wholesome', have become the tools of the advocates of censorship. The last thing I would suggest is that children's reading should be limited to what is good, true and wholesome. One of the greatest benefits to be won from reading is the cultivation of the critical sense; and how are we to develop such a sense, if we read nothing but what is of undisputed moral and literary excellence? If we are tempted to condemn a book a child wishes to read, let us do it subtly by praising a better book; or, better still, by letting the better book speak for itself. In letters, as in nature, for every poison there are many antidotes.

There are certain truths which all of us must learn for ourselves. They must be learned in solitude, in the world of the imagination. We never know when they will come upon us. We cannot seek them, for they are as elusive as sunbeams. Yet they illuminate the world. We catch vanishing glimpses of them:

> Brief as the lightning in the collied night
> That, in a spleen, unfolds both heaven and earth
> And ere a man hath power to say "Behold!"
> The jaws of darkness do devour it up.

One way to these truths is through books. By reading much, comprehending, perhaps, little; but being taken fairly aback now and then with an unaccountable wonder: feeling the tongue of truth flicker among the deeps of childish ignorance. As when, in a seeming wilderness of words, no less magical for being a wilderness, one comes upon:

> Happy in that we are not over happy.
> On fortune's cap we are not the very button.

Or when, drowsy with accumulated rhythm, one feels the brush of beauty and comes full awake with:

> Full many a gem of purest ray serene
> The dark unfathomed caves of ocean bear.

In the world of books these truths spring in utter profusion — and confusion. They are not, perhaps, every man's truths. They do not stand single and straight like trees to be perceived and accepted by all that pass. Often they register upon our consciousness unawares. They may lie dormant and incomplete for years until a phrase, a word, an image brings them perfectly and radiantly to life, and they become henceforth the truths we live by. We may read a book or a poem today and consider that we have profited nothing; yet tomorrow, or next year, or in the contemplative peace of our age, we may happen upon the key that will open at last the reluctant door that conceals "the bright countenance of truth."

The object of reading is to be well read: and the advantages of being well read are countless. One is the development of the critical faculty, already mentioned. Not the mere ability to distinguish a good book from a bad, a masterpiece of painting from a daub, a symphony from a cacophony, but that sovereign power to discriminate, in universal terms, between truth and falsehood, beauty and ugliness, ephemeral and eternal.

Another advantage is the broadening of experience, which leads to deepened understanding. There is no adventure the reader may be denied, no emotional experience he has not access to. What is of ultimate value is not the acquisition of knowledge through the intellect, but the achievement of understanding through the emotions.

A third great benefit of being well read is that of self-expression. Give a child this and you give a treasure without price: for not only does facility with words help to express thought, it stimulates and enhances it.

But perhaps the greatest reward is the awakening of the imagination. Whether we like it or not, man is an imaginative creature, and his road to salvation lies not in seeking to deny the imagination, but in perfecting and using it to the full. If a child does not know the formula for the area of a circle, we need not despair of him. But if he remains unmoved when he hears: "Do not go gentle into that good night..." then are our worst anxieties real. For the chances are that he will stumble unawakened through the world burdened with a life he cannot grasp the meaning of, deprived of all the rich rewards of the spirit, and come to his old age in the sour conviction that life has passed him by.

The Youth Cult

The world of literature is at least in some degree immune to the follies of the "teenage" cult that condemns us interminably to rock stars and the apers of rock stars, to the invasion of our television screens day after day by crowds of children engaged in ungraceful contortions, as though hypnotized, and to vulgarities of dress that are the more vulgar for the slovenliness with which they are imitated.

To practise the art of letters, even in its lowest form, one must have learned a few fundamental things about language and about life. Having won that degree of mastery, it is still necessary to have something of one's own to say: inanity is painfully apparent in print. And once the words are there, they cry one's inadequacies to the world.

In letters, therefore, despite the pressures of modern youth worship, we tend to perpetuate the outworn belief that wisdom and experience are good things, and that they carry authority. There are those who would have us believe youth in a writer to be a virtue that somehow magically enhances his work and renders his sins innocuous; but most of us still demand to see the colour of his intellectual money before we gamble our time and credence upon him. Elsewhere in life we are so anxious not to subscribe to the Victorian belief that children should be seen and not heard, that we stand smiling indulgently while the clamour of undisciplined youth drowns out the voice of reason.

Once, youth deferred to the wisdom of age. It was thus for many centuries. Civilization was founded upon the principle that one comes into the world knowing nothing; that knowledge is acquired only slowly and by apprehension of the external world through the senses; and that until it has acquired enough such knowledge for its protection and advancement, the human animal must be shielded from the consequences of its ignorance and folly. It took man many ages to learn that he could pass on the little discoveries of his life to those that came after him, to emerge from that primitive state where every man's wisdom died with him; where generation repeated the mistakes of generation and where every man, beginning the journey of life from the same point, made the same faltering steps towards understanding, only to die intellectually intestate. But in time age came to be venerated for its wisdom. In the ancient civilizations of the East, this deference was carried to the point where the young not only counted it a privilege to serve their elders and to be instructed by them, but looked upon their superior station with envy. Far from dreading the advance of years, youth looked forward with joy to the access of wisdom and the respect it would bring.

How different from this age of ours, when the young, lacking the courage and imagination to face the prospect of their own old age, fear what they will not confront, and are contemptuous of what they fear. I was recently told by an undergraduate that the chief concern of most students is with "security". Their sense of adventure, this would suggest, is dead. Devoid of gratitude to their elders for the past, of respect in the present, and of discernment concerning the future, they are completely unaware that the only true security is the security of being, in the broadest possible sense, loved; the security of knowing that there will always be a succouring hand, a responsive heart, a Samaritan deed. And so we march onward to the welfare state, never asking ourselves whether in trying to legislate the public conscience we may not be perhaps destroying the very thing we seek to create.

In our world the accent everywhere is on youth. Our lives are increasingly regulated by the need to cater to the whims and safeguard the sensibilities of the young, to avoid violence to their freedom or threat to their natural development. They are the makers of tomorrow. We must not, we ignorant and selfish oldsters, interfere with their great and sovereign destiny. Why should we be allowed to meddle in a world not we but they shall inhabit? All the ills of today's world occurred under the leadership of the mature, the argument goes: obviously the solution is to relinquish control to the immature. What a perilous fallacy! It is as if, dissatisfied with the state of contemporary justice, we elected to let a child try a man for his life.

We have all come to regard this reverence for youth as inevitable and right, but is it? Should we not stop deluding ourselves and squarely confront the fact that youth is merely a formative time, a period of disciplined apprenticeship for life; and that the more bewilderingly complex life becomes, the greater becomes the need for discipline and wise counsel?

But youth must learn the practice of its democratic responsibility, the advanced thinkers say, as if believing that the short road to democracy lies through anarchy and indiscipline. Youth has its own wisdom, but it also has its follies. The wisdom is not well served by indulging the follies. We shall not arrive at mature democracy, at true government by the people, by shirking our responsibility for producing people capable of governing themselves. Democracy is the greatest of all disciplines. How will they ever practise discipline, who have never known it?

Today we hear it said that the older generation is out of touch with the new knowledge (meaning the latest advances in technology) and is not therefore capable of leading. Before we swallow this dangerous doctrine we should get clear in our minds what knowledge it is they need who are to be the arbiters of the world's destiny. I speak not of statesmen merely, but of all those who by their leadership, influence and example determine the shape and direction of things to come. It is no new knowledge that in the crisis of our civilization will save and vindicate it, but the full understanding and wise application of the old, the primeval knowledge. We have, God knows, more knowledge than we can comfortably stomach now. What a surfeited man needs is not to eat more, but to digest a little.

3

Art and Attitudes

Beauty and Utility

"We should do our utmost to encourage the beautiful," wrote Goethe, "for the useful encourages itself."

In material matters we are much more susceptible to the potency of this truth than we were in Goethe's day. We are less tolerant of the needlessly ugly, and we prefer the useful to be beautiful so long as it costs us nothing. But we still, most of us, lead ugly lives, are still submissive to an ugly society, still tolerate ugliness in politics and in our human relations. We wallow in ugly ideas, ugly behaviour, ugly attitudes, ugly appetites and ugly ambitions. We grow ugly and stunted in our souls. And we are never more culpable than when we accept ugliness as inevitable; when we turn a Nelsonian eye to it, shirk our responsibility for it and ascribe it to human nature, as if our own nature and its consequences were not our most immediate and solemn concern.

Critics are apt to apologize for Keats, who said much the same things as Goethe but stuck out his elegant neck still further. It is not quite precise, they imply, to say that "Beauty is truth, truth beauty." Keats did not mean quite that. Did he not, indeed! He meant it, every glowing trenchant word. He meant that what is good and true appeals not to our moral but to our aesthetic sense. He meant that evil invariably manifests itself in some form of ugliness. He meant that if we concerted all our prodigious energies toward the beautiful, truth would take care of itself.

When we fall short of the ideal, we recognize it through the same sensitive and perfectible antennae of discrimination by which we detect the second-rate or the spurious in literature, the discordant in music, the unlovely in art. When we countenance the imperfect, turn away our eyes from frailty and declare it none of our concern, do a mean when we might do a noble thing, we feel ourselves grow ugly inside. For the sense of beauty is but a sense of rightness; of rightness exalted and refined, appealing not to sluggard reason but to the warm, quick, wonder-aware emotions.

It is possibly demonstrable that a city or a country or a world comes in time to reflect the soul-ugliness of its inhabitants, as surely as human bodies do. We have little cause for complacency while slums proliferate, while heaps of derelict cars defile the countryside, while advertising, of taste commensurate with its honesty, spreads over the scene like a rash.

But all this is only symptomatic. The attitude that Goethe sought by his words to engender is the important thing: the attitude of true and courageous criticism that would submit all things and all thoughts to the arbitration of the aesthetic conscience. It is an attitude that would select always that which is beautiful (that is, true, noble, virtuous) over that which is ugly (that is, false, evil, tawdry, immoral): and it calls for a continuing affirmation of faith, for the benefits are not previously demonstrable. The beautiful always demands a little more effort, and there is always some expediency or utility to argue against that effort.

It is only what we put into anything beyond the necessary minimum that reaps a true reward. When a thing is made, it is only when it is wrought upon with love beyond the demands of mere utility that it begins to attain value and significance. When a deed is done or a decision taken, it is only to the extent that the expedient is subordinated to the beautiful — the immediate and selfish, that is, to the universal — that we feel ourselves enriched and ennobled thereby, that we grow and are truly fulfilled.

There is no excuse for ugliness in art. The act of creation that is not a striving after beauty, in the broad sense that I have indicated, is an abomination. There may be works of art treating of life's uglinesses, but there should not be — must not be, if art is to retain any vestige of sanity — ugly works of art. A biography may hold up to view an ugly life, a portrait an ugly person, but they had best be beautiful about it. Stevenson's essay on François Villon is a prime example.

In the act of creation a man is alone with his aesthetic faculty. None but his own infirmities becloud his glorious lucidity, impede his fleet pursuit of the ideal. He must accept full responsibility for his ugly failures, his ugly pseudo-successes, his ugly mediocrities. Above all is he culpable in any concession to utility at the expense of beauty, in serving any but what he knows in his deepest heart to be the true end, whether the lure be fame, money, power or ease unearned.

However practical our purpose, it is always incumbent upon us to discharge that intention beautifully. It is at our most utilitarian that we are most in need of Goethe's truth. If we are but describing how to make a table, can we not at least enter into it with warmth, do it as though we love the doing? Izaak Walton stands as an eternal reminder that utility is best served when it is beautifully served.

Could we but bring ourselves to accept this truth and submit to be lit on our way by it, whether we would be about building a new wall or a new world, how much more often we might break the spell that binds captive, in Utility's beastly guise, that handsome prince, Perfection.

Literature and the Law

Inevitably, and fortunately, the law is slow to adapt to social change. It lags behind the modes of morality, and is always a little out of phase with the pendulum-swing of popular opinion. Were this not so, we should be at the mercy of mob indignation and prudery on the march. Something little better than lynch law would prevail. Every outburst of popular displeasure would be reflected in a succession of ephemeral laws, replete with good intentions but devoid of justice. Laws are the calm afterthoughts of accumulated experience: they yield to empirical wisdom rather than to present exigencies, and hence they are stable and largely resistant to human passion and inhuman guile.

But as the price of stability we must accept the opposite risk, that the laggard law will be exploited by the forces of reaction to retard progress and delay enlightenment. Statutes that are a little conservative in their philosophy or a little woolly in their wording become the tools of the illiberal and the retroverted. They will be used by those whose moral zeal exceeds their good sense to interfere with the freedom they were framed to protect.

This infirmity of the law has been nowhere more apparent than in the long battle to emancipate literature from the toils of censorship. Great books have been maligned and stigmatized, great and good people have been persecuted because the law in its attempts to suppress what we know today as "hard core pornography" has lent itself by default to abuse by puritanical judges and vociferous minorities.

One has but to mention the names of Havelock Ellis, D.H. Lawrence, Flaubert, Walt Whitman and Margaret Sanger — names taken at random from the long list of the persecuted — to show the reality and extent of the menace. One has but to point a finger at the activities of Anthony Comstock, who over a period of forty years was to American morality what McCarthy later became to American politics, to demonstrate the vulnerability of writers and publishers to the abuse of vague laws.

Comstock, whose maxim was "Morals, not art and literature," proceeded on the principle that proof of "possible harm to a child" was sufficient ground for conviction. The idiocy of this doctrine is so apparent that we look back upon it with complacency and even with amused condescension as something that couldn't happen in our enlightened age. Yet Comstock terrorized the American publishing industry and joyfully drove more than one victim of his witch hunt to suicide, under the aegis of laws not much different from our own.

A Canadian Comstock, borne into power by misguided moral zealots and fanatical pressure groups, abetted by a few judges and magistrates of like temper, and ignored until too late by a notoriously apathetic public, could flourish in our midst today.

The U.S. law of Comstock's time was still founded substantially upon a pronouncement of Lord Chief Justice Cockburn in England in 1867:

The test of obscenity is this, whether the tendency of the matter charged as obscene is to deprave and corrupt those whose minds are open to such immoral influences and into whose hands a publication of this sort may fall.

This definition contains two open invitations to unscrupulous prudery. It suggests that anything is obscene which excites obscene thoughts in minds with a natural tendency to depravity, and invites the use of such sick minds as a sort of litmus to determine what the rest of the community may read. This is no more reasonable than decreeing that no one may eat fat because some people have jaundice, and because "all looks yellow to the jaundiced eye."

Equally indefensible is the suggestion that literary works should be suppressed if there is a possibility of their falling into improper hands. "Improper hands" fall presumably into two categories: the perverted and the youthful. The perverted or readily perverted are like drug addicts and will seek out their unsavoury fare regardless of the law and the climate of morality. The young will not concern themselves with it unless it is thrust upon their notice, through either carelessness or design.

Moral crusaders have still to learn the lesson of Prohibition, that the illicit tempts the adventurous, that men value freedom even above virtue. He only is virtuous who is virtuous by choice: no one was ever yet bundled into heaven in a straitjacket. To catch that fragile creature Morality, one needs a delicate net indeed.

Canadian law is a little more advanced —in intent if not in susceptibility to abuse — than that under which Comstockery prospered; and in the recent years it has been applied with restraint. Indeed, successive governments, believing apparently that what is important is not the letter of the law but its interpretation, that good judges are preferable to good laws, have been more than happy to let the sleeping dog of censorship lie. The official attitude seems to be that so long as the attention of the groups of moral busybodies is engaged elsewhere, the government is content to forget that the obscenity law is still an ass, albeit a sleeping one.

The Postmaster General and the Minister of National Revenue are equally happy not to be reminded that they hold Comstockian powers no less terrifying for their desuetude, powers little short of totalitarian.

Mr. Nicholson's assertion that "No government can legislate people's tastes and preferences," even though made in another, less admirable connection, is reassuring. But when the basic freedoms are involved, it is questionable whether benevolent forbearance is enough. In such circumstances one can only be as benevolent, and can only be benevolent for as long, as the militant forces of Grundyism in the community will allow.

Note:

I was misguided enough, at the time of writing "Literature and the Law," to refer to "the sleeping dogs of censorship" in Canada. Not long afterwards, those dogs awoke with a vengeance and began snapping and snarling at the heels of some of Canada's most distinguished writers. Among the persecuted were that most gentle and admirable of men, Ernest Buckler, and Margaret Laurence, a woman whose generous spirit and probity her detractors would do well to emulate. The ground on which the work of these writers was attacked was precisely that of which I had said that its idiocy was so apparent that we could look back upon it with complacency and even with amused condescension, namely, that of "possible harm to a child." Anyone who has read The Mountain and the Valley *cannot but conclude that "idiocy" is far too mild a word.*

Since then, also, a new bureaucratic ogre has emerged to menace our freedom of expression. Canadian customs officers are now arbiters of literary taste and keepers of the public morals. Not only may they deny entry of any publication into the country, but they may seize all copies without so much as turning a page.

Clearly the warning contained in my second paragraph is still as relevant as when I wrote it.

Prudery and the Pen

It was tame as paperback covers go: a female body from the lower swell of the breasts down to the vicinity of the ankles, with a strategically placed white square containing a fig leaf. There are perhaps disturbing inferences to be drawn (which I deny) from the fact that it was not the cover of the book that beguiled me, but its title — *Mrs. Grundy: Studies in English Prudery*. A fascinating and rewarding book, but I found that it supplied me with a question rather than an answer. But perhaps that is what a book should do.

What is prudery, and why are we plagued with it? You may share my surprise — and join in my immediate "of course" — at the discovery that the dictionary limits this vice and traces its origin to the female sex. A prude, it says unequivocally, is a "woman of extreme (esp. affected) propriety in conduct or speech." Much as one (a masculine one, that is) would like to believe this, if there is anything proved by Peter Fryer's book it is that this curse, though it may have been invented by women, is certainly not limited to them in its practice. In its most pernicious forms, however, it is usually in some way associated with women, and I suspect that it became a vice because they exploited it for purposes anything but proper, in the dictionary's sense.

Since prudery is the mother of censorship, which to a writer is abhorrent in any form, it is easy to sympathize with Mr. Fryer in his assumption that prudery always, and in all its forms, is bad. It is easy until one remembers some of the admirable people who are prudes within Mr. Fryer's implied definition. The most ardent reader of Henry Miller who balks at emulating Miller's freedom of language in the presence of ladies — is he not as much a prude as the Victorian dames in America who veiled the seductive shape of their chairlegs in frilly drawers?

The prudish attitude having once prevailed in connection with any word, idea, thing or mode of behaviour, conformity with that attitude becomes a matter of good taste. Taboos can be invented only by narrow and nasty minds, but they flourish by the sanction of people of sensitivity and goodwill. Once suggest to such persons that a word is indelicate, whether they consider it so or not, and they will refrain from using it for fear of giving offence: for the essence of good manners is to avoid doing violence to the sensibilities of others. Prudery being altogether a paradoxical infirmity, the bad person's vice becomes thus the good person's virtue.

It seems likely that the beginnings of prudery were several. When people started covering themselves, for protection rather than concealment, it would not be long before that which was hidden took upon itself a mystery. Another strong influence was doubtless the instinctive desire to conceal ugliness. This is a potent human motive, especially when the ugliness is one's own. A woman no longer young and shapely might well seek to retain her allure by concealing and embellishing her deficiencies, and then make by moral suasion a virtue of her sad necessity. Nor would it take her long, in a world of ignorance and superstition, to discover that mystery is power.

It is but a small step to the point where that which may not be seen may not even be named. And so begins the endless cycle of euphemisms and obliquities that persists over the centuries, while the things themselves annoyingly and blessedly remain ("Isn't life a terrible thing, thank God!" says Dylan Thomas's Polly Garter), and the original earthy names of them flourish beneath the surface of propriety, outliving all their seedy adversaries and mocking all attempts to express otherwise the things they express so well.

Of course there are fashions in prudery. At some times language is the butt; at others, dress; at still others, behaviour. In one age, a bull must be called a gentleman cow; in another, we must clothe Cupid. Today we may regard the bosom: tomorrow, not an ankle.

This situation has resulted from the acceptance by writers and artists of the responsibility for fostering true broadmindedness. From this it might appear that one of their functions is to shock, and some of them have embraced this function with more glee than finesse. But although it may be somewhat of an overstatement to say that art should shock, it is certainly incumbent upon writers and artists to struggle free of preconceptions, and to remain sceptical of conventions that have no foundation but in convention itself.

Perhaps the only way to break down the final barriers of prudery in language would be for a determined few to assail them on the platforms of public speech as D.H. Lawrence and Henry Miller assailed them in literature: but the effectiveness — and the safety — of such a course are doubtful. Society, it seems, is not capable of containing the pressures of prudery: they must out. Contained at one point, they will forcibly emerge at another. But in literature at least we now have a point of reference with the absolute. As readers in our armchairs we can smile tolerantly at our prudish other selves clowning it so seriously in the social swim.

The Illusion of Progress

In the midst of my rejoicing as the astronauts splashed safely into the Atlantic, a small impertinent voice deep down wanted suddenly and insistently to know what was the purpose of it all.

Progress, I said, glueing my ear to the radio.

Towards what? the small voice said. Yesterday man hopped a few North Carolina hedges. Today he leaps at the stars. Tomorrow — who knows? But why?

That's progress, I said again, getting irritable.

Progress implies motion towards something. Something not necessarily known but at least wholeheartedly believed in, and to some extent deducible from the consistency of the progress towards it. You can't have progress without a goal: only change.

The small voice was warming to it. I switched off the radio.

Change, like falsehood, feeds upon itself. Changes, like lies, must often be multiplied to sustain themselves. "That word 'change'," said Haliburton, "is the incantation that calls fools into a circle." More, unfortunately, than that: it leads wise men in a circle. Mistaking change for progress, they gyrate through the wilderness of their delusion like men lost in the woods at nightfall.

Since man began in a state of nature, it follows that all change tends away from nature and towards artificiality: which brief reflection will show to be basically unsound and beyond certain limits ignoble.

So, I said, you want man to go back to his rude simplicity, to some primitive Golden Age.

No, but I suggest that he is retreating daily farther from all possibility of any sort of Golden Age; that somewhere along the line of his "advance" he has widely missed it, as his shots at the stars sometimes go swinging off into space beyond all hope of recovery or control. And for much the same reasons. The star of destiny which philosopher man occasionally glimpses through the clouds changes its position constantly in relation to the world on which he plants his feet to leap. Things must be known to such a nicety that, at the point of nearest proximity, the momentum of advance will not exceed the attraction of the target. Today, man is obsessed with the rate of his "progress", but he has little regard for its direction.

You exaggerate, I said.

Then you defend a "civilizing" process that made an anachronism of your mother's milk before it was dry upon your lips? You are optimistic about a future in which bodies will grow ugly, obese and inept while machines do magnificently, precisely and with incredible rapidity things which do not, if we are fundamentally honest, need doing? The nightmare vision of machines assuming control of man's destiny has been the theme of many a far-fetched tale; yet has not the machine, in a way more subtle than any of those tales envisaged, done just that? We grow so reliant upon human ingenuity for survival that we may well regret that man, "Binding nature fast in fate, left free the human will." For man has so misused his will as to be in danger of depriving himself of it, and the subjugation of nature which he undertook for his own preservation bids fair to destroy him. The moral of this is of course that all excess is evil, even excess of good. Progress can degenerate, just as kindness can kill. Why after all is it so urgently desirable a thing to people the planets with ludicrously bedizened men?

Knowledge, I said. Such ventures are an invaluable source of scientific data that will be of great benefit in further exploration of the universe.

But is this not perhaps a mere morbid addiction to scientific knowledge? Is this more admirable than the acquisition of money with no other object than to multiply it? Money and knowledge are both means, not ends. The perversion of means into ends is the shrewdest weapon of the Devil. The sole object of knowledge is understanding: and how little of that there is current in this world. Yet given only this, all things are possible. Without it, all knowledge is vanity, all progress mockery, all aspiration impertinence.

The more man complicates his material life, the more difficult must become the solution to his basic problems, and the more reluctant he becomes to face them, even to acknowledge that they exist. Do we ever pause to ask what the ideal state of human existence is, to which we should be progressing? Dare we ask that question now, when the answer may well be, "Too late!"?

Many are the benefits we imagine ourselves to have reaped from "progress", but it is becoming increasingly clear that these are largely illusory. Have we ever paused to consider that if all the drawbacks of life which we labour so immensely to eliminate were in truth removed, life itself would become meaningless? The very nature of man and his world ensures that, as he removes one thorn of discomfort from his flesh, another inevitably appears. This is not as pessimistic a statement as it may seem, for pleasure draws most of its savour from the possibility of pain. And since it is impossible to eliminate discomfort, we might profitably pay more attention to enduring it with dignity, and less to devising means of exchanging one form of it for another.

Through the ages man has striven tirelessly to order material things to his liking. But seldom has he paused, as any good soldier will tell you he should, to consolidate his position before pushing on to new conquests. He has laboured unceasingly to adapt the world to himself: now, before it is too late, he must learn to adapt himself to the world.

Yes, I said wearily, but...

The small voice emitted only a sigh.

Taste to Order

It is not easy, looking back, to decide which of the many books we devoured so gluttonously in youth were the truly potent forces in shaping us. Even less easy to determine why and how, for it is hard to be truthful. Not of course that we incline more to falsehood than most: it is simply that we are no longer the same persons. We have learnt a little and experienced much, and although not necessarily wiser we are assuredly less naive. And however diligently we study to avoid it, we shall be prone to ascribe to the avid, indiscriminate mind of youth all the preferences and finer faculties we now possess.

Could we but make that leap back to innocence and candour, we should no doubt find that it was by no means the best books that had the most profound effects, that their influence was as obvious as it was deep, and the results of that influence as surprising as they were extensive. I have a conviction that those influences were almost wholly good, and that even atrociously bad books do not, as the censor-morons suggest, corrupt us. But such influences are subtle, and so enormously complicated by their action one upon another that the result is a psychiatrist's nightmare. That last is a roguishly pleasant thought, for psychiatrists that meddle in the world of books deserve all the nightmares they get. No doubt psychiatrists have their place. One hopes it is not too hot for their comfort. Certainly, though, that place is not in the pleasant bookish cloisters of the mind, where, like vivisectionists, they can come at knowledge only by destroying what they seek to know.

But how shamefully we digress! I set out to remark that I was profoundly influenced, many years ago, by a book of Arnold Bennett's called *Literary Taste: How to form it*. The decision to make such an observation was innocent of psychological intention, and had but a small ingredient of senile reminiscence. It was simply that the title struck me suddenly as quaint, even archaic, and that this quaintness was in some way significant.

The book was written, I believe, shortly before the First World War. At the time I read it, it had sprouted a new edition after the customary period of post-publication eclipse, and enjoyed for a time an Indian summer of critical acclaim. In all probability it is now out of print, and my object is certainly not to advocate its reissue: for however much one may admire Bennett and however laudable may have been his intention, one cannot but have misgivings about any attempt to inculcate taste in cold blood. It is but one step further to the folly of *Poetry Made Simple*.

I remember little of what the author said, but the overall impression remains, and despite what I have just said I have the conviction that the book was very wise and very practical without in any way prejudicing the integrity and the idealism such a fine writer could not but possess. It would convert no Philistines, for the obvious reason that no Philistine would read it, but for one who already loved books to the point of obsession it was a welcome embodiment of things ardently felt but only dimly discerned. It was a chart of miraculous seas for one just setting forth with all the high optimism of a Vasco da Gama. I read it in somewhat the same spirit that the obese, in these diet-obsessed days, devour books assuring them they can grow slim without curbing their appetite or shaking off their indolence.

I don't recall that there was any attempt to define what literary taste is, or was. I remember the happy conceit that acquiring it is like learning to ride a bicycle: so awkward and seemingly impossible at first that we are convinced that those who profess to enjoy it are liars. But very soon the effort diminishes and we have attention to spare for the delights of the countryside. At any rate, the concept of literary taste seemed eminently reasonable to me. I had no doubt that such a thing existed, and the book left me with a sufficiently distinct and lasting idea of its nature for me to gravely question, now, whether we still possess it; whether, like other values that tend to raise uncomfortable questions in this slick computer age, it is simply ceasing to exist. The words themselves, certainly, are no longer fashionable, or even meaningful.

If we leave aside a certain Victorian aftertaste of dilettantism and intellectual snobbery, a suggestion of remoteness from the bitter realities of living that might make the words distasteful to us now — just as, through abuse and over-use, the word "culture" is becoming distasteful — there still remains the question whether the idea the words represented still exists. It seems to me that we no longer have the attitude to literature and to life that the book's title reflects.

Today we may "like books," be "great readers" or even have "a taste for books," but even this last is a very different thing from what Bennett had in mind when he spoke of literary taste. We no longer conceive of literature as an entity, as a quality that all good books possess in common as an attribute quite distinct from — though born of — the excellence of their content; as something for which one can and should acquire a taste that has nothing to do with one's hunger for knowledge or one's desire not to appear ignorant in society. If the concept of literary taste does still exist, those who educate the new generations of students in "English literature" are content to ignore it in their preoccupation with the "message" alleged to be implicit in the books they examine. Similarly, the massive reading programs, the book clubs that would fill our shelves with handsomely bound classics, variously appeal to our desire to know more or to our sense of guilt that we do not; to our feeling of social inferiority, to our acquisitive greed, or simply to that dreamy part of us that hazily aspires to perfect itself. None of them seeks to satisfy, much less to inculcate, literary taste.

But what is most lamentable, and what remains evident when all the dubious connotations of the phrase are disposed of, is that literary taste is no longer operative as a standard of criticism.

Quiller on the Couch

One can only think with regret of the days when a man could follow a profession or an art or a caprice simply because it was his will and pleasure. It is hard to believe there was a time when a man might write a book or paint a picture without being called to psychological account for it, without being compelled to wonder why he did it. That he wanted to was reason enough, and though he might be burnt in the market place he was never publicly dissected there. What he produced was anyone's prey, but his motives and mechanisms were inviolate.

Medicine in general has always drawn a discreet esoteric screen around its mysteries. It has never insisted, for example, that a man must be familiar with all the miraculous but unappetizing workings of his digestion before he can enjoy his food. The psychological sciences, however, tend to exhibitionism. From using works of art to deduce the character of their creators and the influences by which that character was formed, they very soon began to trespass upon the fields of criticism. The focus of their interest shifted from the man, of whose inner workings and emotional bruises the work was symptomatic, to the work itself, with the man and all his foibles as the key, its dull and dusty concordance.

Some of them even went so far, when their interpretations and profound symbologies were challenged by the authors of the works they sought to explain, as to imply condescendingly that the authors did not know what they were talking about. A wise author would await their analysis before deciding what he had said, or even what he had intended to say.

All of which we learned grudgingly to tolerate. A man is not, surprisingly, shocked into silence by the thought that the lightest words of his pen are perhaps betraying a morbid, though unsuspected, attraction to his mother. The painter's brush arm is not frozen by contemplation of the secrets every stroke reveals. Though doubtless pen and brush are subtly diverted. And who knows but that the antics and wild oddities of the younger aspirants to the arts are the indirect result of all these induced notions concerning the character of the artist and the sort of experience out of which art grows? I offer this as a fruitful field of study for our psychocentric friends, to determine to what extent the course of art has been changed by their interest. Or, on a broader scale, in what measure history is deflected by man's awareness of himself naked and transparent upon the great diagnostic couch of the world.

All of which, as I began to say, the artist came to accept with good humour and sometimes even with a few grace-notes for the gallery. He tolerated it because he was prompted by simple curiosity. He might not agree with Dr. Johnson that it is one of the nobler faculties of man, but he was naive enough to believe that curiosity could be simple, devoid of motive.

When a man becomes curious about something, it is never long before he begins to ask, "What use can I make of it?" It seems to him a shocking waste that anything should exist purely for its own sake. And so now the vultures of industry wheel and alight on the treetops, eyeing hungrily the "creative people" who falter from thirst in the cultural wilderness. They are inciting research to discover what makes the clock of creativity tick, so that it may be made to tick for their profit and win a place for their portraits in the boardrooms of posterity.

What futility. Is it not evident that the first reaction of any person who is creative in any true sense of that hackneyed word will shy away from them? To the extent that a man is creative, to that same extent will he be inaccessible to their blandishments. The creative spirit is diminished by greed, luxury, lack of real challenge. It cannot be bought or sold. To be creative is simply to be free; free to do those things which our deepest prompting tell us are most worth doing. When you buy a man's freedom of expression he becomes simply another slave. Why ask a man of vision to behave like one blind, or a person sound of limb to affect a crippled gait? Ah, the lords of industry say in effect, but how much more adroitly a man with sight might wield a white cane or manage a guide dog! How agile an athlete would be upon crutches!

It is surprising that all this research into the "creative personality" did not discover among its dominant characteristics an aversion to the sort of moral slavery industry imposes. To be creative is to wish to create, with words, pigments, sounds or any other medium; and the wish is fulfilled to the degree that one is faithful to it, to the determination with which one turns away from all temptation to betray it.

Fiction and History

"The novelist who chooses to set his book in a past age," wrote Jay Williams, "is in a difficult position." Just how difficult, even Mr. Williams fails to appreciate, for although he doggedly defends the historical novel as a legitimate form of art, and ably demolishes other people's attempts to prove it is not one, he seems singularly unaware of the true reasons why, as he puts it, "the novel about the past has been considered a minor sort of art, something like genre painting…it being understood that such a work could never really be 'literature'."

Having come thus unwittingly close to the truth, Mr. Williams immediately lost sight of it, and settled for the contention that historical fiction was emasculated as an art form by the flood of historical romances that were produced to satisfy the demands of newly literate "emancipated women with money to spend on books and time for reading, but a taste, unfortunately, that ran to candy rather than claret." This saccharine stuff was the spawning bed of the "movie spectacular", and Mr. Williams believes that all historical fiction is condemned without trial today because of these dubious antecedents. Prejudice on this account there may well be, but I do not believe that the validity of any art was ever diminished or destroyed by abuse. The potency of an art form is not lessened for its true practitioners because it has been exploited to the point of nausea by quacks or incompetents. How sorry would be the plight of poetry, were this true. Nor can I believe that all critics are so bigoted as to be incapable of recognizing a great novel about the past, should such a rarity appear, merely on account of the sins of Sabatini and the vulgarities of Cecil B. de Mille.

A *New Yorker* reviewer went equally wide of the mark when he contended that there can be no such things as a good historical novel because no one can satisfactorily reconstruct the past. Reconstructing the past is the historian's job, not the novelist's, but it is not true to say that this thing cannot be done because it so seldom is.

The truth is, I suspect, that the characteristics of a great historian and a great novelist are virtually incompatible: or, rather, that the emotional and intellectual resources that must be drawn upon to produce a great novel preclude access to those required for the writing of great history. Speaking nostalgically of the early novelists (unburdened by the memory of the emancipated women), Mr. Williams said: "All that was demanded of him was that he write the best book that was in him." Herein lies the secret. To write the best novel that is in him, an author must be free to concede to any demands made by that novel, both upon himself and upon the material. If fact or chronology impose a constraint upon him, then it must go out of the window, and his reputation among the historical fraternity with it.

The historian owes his first allegiance to his external sources: the novelist, like the poet, to those wayward and intuitive sources within. He truly writes the best book that is in him, and he is likely to write a great novel that is unimpeachable history only if the past with which he deals is so completely assimilated that he can draw upon it as naturally and spontaneously as he draws upon the memories of his childhood: and then only if, in its unaltered state, it best suits his purpose. His novel can only grow out of himself, and only by organic growth out of its own beginnings.

Research and verification are things extraneous to the novelist's most pressing purpose, and unless they are done and forgotten before his work has need of them they will mar the finished book, as scaffolding would do if it somehow became incorporated into the building it was used to erect, as they mar many a modern historical novel.

It is for the same reasons that one rarely comes across a work of science fiction that is truly significant as literature: the difficulties that beset the novelist who ventures into the past pursue him also into any seriously prophetic sally into the future. And, indeed, into any finnickingly realistic appraisal of the present: realistic, that is, in the sense that he feels obliged to gather material for his book by conscious and clinical effort, like a royal commission.

A work of literature in the making has its own organic necessities. It cannot achieve greatness by the slavish depicting of externals, any more than a painting can. Immediately one accepts the primary purpose of the art, one acknowledges the need to make all else subservient to that purpose. A painter, for example, dare not consider himself bound by the fact that a tree's foliage is of a particular shade of green, if to paint it so would not be true to his artistic intention, or if it spoiled the colour composition of his painting: and in any case, the chances are that by painting it blue he can more truly convey the reality of the tree than by meticulous imitation of its natural pigment.

One has but to read the statements of the greater novelists about how their works were born, and how they grew, to realize why a book that is at the same time valid as history and significant as a novel is not only rare but almost freakish. All the influences that bear upon a novelist, both from without and from within, help in the shaping of his work, and no one, not even the author himself, can predict what it will become until it is finished. It must come to life and it must mature to its own perfection in the environment of its author's personality and experience. This is why (since Jay Williams demands, a little belligerently, to know) "the profound and sombre medieval novels of Zoe Oldenburg (are) shrugged off by literary critics...while the egotistical pornography of Henry Miller is regarded with reverence."

There will always be novelists who will succumb to the fascination of the past, in the belief that the drudgery of the research and the strait-jacket of recorded fact are worth enduring on account of the fertility of the terrain; but for most, all this represents an unprofitable expenditure of creative energy and imposes a needless temptation to compromise. Why incur so dead a burden, when there is such a wealth of material so much more ready to hand?

Art and Individuality

Courage ranks high among the attributes of art. What distinguishes the masterpiece from the brilliantly mediocre is merely that it has the courage to be itself. It is for this reason that Irving Layton is such a significant figure in the history of Canadian literature. It has nothing to do with the stature of his work. Only time will decide that. He is important because it was he above all who awakened the conscience of Canadian poetry: reminded his brothers of the pen what they should be about, and asserted the need for courageous independence. "I wanted," he wrote, "to give a truthful account of the world as I experienced it." Simply that. A child could do it. Children are doing it all the time. But in a man it takes the highest kind of courage and more than a tincture of genius. To lead, not to follow popular thought. Not with any vainglorious thought of leading. Not with arrogance. Not with flaming sword and shouts of "Follow me!" But simply and unassumingly making one's own way, letting follow who will. Layton erred here. He was too aware of his mission, too conscious of the burden of leadership. What he did suffered because of over-concern with why he did it.

He had courage to do what was in him crying out to be done, undeterred by all questions of "propriety", by all the inhibitions that flock aloft with great commotion of wings as soon as a person sets foot in the wilderness of literary creation. But he tended to make sport of it. He went forth with beaters and bird-dogs flushing the coveys of convention: arriving perhaps not at the highest pinnacle of accomplishment, but having good hunting along the way.

All of which commands our indulgence. Mr. Layton's extravagances are mere peccadilloes compared to the sins of the slaves of convention, for whom the applause of their neighbours is sweeter than the approbation of their artistic conscience. If a man think always within the pale of convention, how shall he have means of assessing that convention's validity? If you enclose a man in a box with no window upon the world, by what reference point is he to know that the box imperceptibly but inexorably shrinks, and he with it? But if bondage to conventional thought has its dangers, if the refusal to countenance any idea that was not acceptable to our grandmothers is destructive to our culture, how much more perilous is the spurious cult of originality. Because by the painstaking study of the works of the great, a few diligent researchers in every generation arrive at the obvious — namely, that every work of genius is different from anything that was ever done before — originality itself attains the stature of a virtue. It is no longer a property a work possesses because it is the fearless unique testament of an individual, but something added to it by the pinch, the teaspoon or the bucketful, according to one's audacity and one's publisher's estimate of the public temper.

Be original, we are told. From the veriest quack who would teach us to write in twelve easy — but expensive — lessons, to the sagest critic, they urge it upon us. We know there is nothing new under the sun, they say, but at least say it in a new way.

Be original! As if one could put on originality like a new coat. Or, if possessed of it, one could shed it, like a snake its skin. As well admonish a man, be tall! Be handsome! Be a genius! And on account of this constant exhortation to originality, we see around us writers ignoring their own original talent to perform like dancing bears in the circus of literature. Some of them attain considerable repute by destroying idols or exposing scandals: not to be altruistic but to be original.

The writer of true stature is he who survives all this blandishment and ballyhoo to discover at last that the only way to be original is to be natural, to be oneself. Originality is something each of us possesses simply by virtue of being a person, a consciousness islanded in its own peculiar relationship to space and time. Nothing new under the sun? I am new. I am unique. I never existed before. Never before was life seen from exactly where I stand. If I look around or within me and do my workmanlike best to make literature out of what I perceive, how can I fail to be original? "A poet," Mr. Layton more succinctly puts it, "is someone who has a strong sense of self and feels his life to be meaningful."

It is a strange but demonstrable truth that through this awareness of self one arrives at an understanding of others. Deep within the shell of his uniqueness, each of us secretes a precious essence of humanity. How else can I know the workings of a man but by looking within myself? I cannot go about opening men up like oysters to discover what they contain, but I know only too well what chafes in my own consciousness. I need but the courage to believe it a pearl: a substance at my centre true and precious and of great beauty, that I have in common with all men; such that when through art I attain to it, the result will be so original that every reader will say, "Why, that's exactly what I've always thought."

"In every work of genius," say Emerson, "we see our own rejected thoughts." We all have our pearl. All we need is the courage.

Ill-Literacy

In reporting conditions in "under-developed" parts of the world, the various philanthropic agencies are accustomed to speak of famine, pestilence and illiteracy in the same awed and admonitory tone, as if these were calamities of equal magnitude; as if to be unlettered were as great an affliction as to be unfed, or as if to allow men to live in ignorance of abstract things we consider important were as gross a shame upon the public conscience as to allow them to die in agony. On the evidence of history it would be hard to justify this concern for the misfortunes of the illiterate, and when one fairly appraises the state of our own society it is equally hard not to be sceptical about the benefits of mass education.

The fallacy lies in regarding literacy itself as a virtue, and in esteeming it for its own sake rather than for the uses to which it can be put and the miracles it makes possible. It is no shame for a man to be illiterate in a barbaric society, nor is barbarism itself a shame. Despite the cynics and the civilization-mongers of our generation the concept of the noble savage is not an invalid one. We have been too long under the misapprehension that to be civilized is to be artificial, to be "industrialized", to be as far removed from nature as possible. What is shameful is to be culturally sterile in a literate society, to pervert the gift of literacy to narrow or sordid purposes. Is it not better to be innocent of knowledge than to apply it to corrupt ends?

Today, that which cannot be bent to material ends is little regarded. Literacy is valued not for the opportunity it offers us to ennoble ourselves but for its power to abet us in our baseness. Is that man truly more admirable than the headhunter or the taker of scalps, who uses his education to enslave or rob or corrupt his fellows? Perhaps it is folly in me to suggest that he who carves a soapstone seal and reads never a word is a more noble and valuable member of the human race than he who uses a university education to write spurious advertising copy, but I am convinced it is true. There are countless examples in our society of this misuse of literacy, so that instead of being the key to learning, wisdom and true civilization, it becomes the tool of the selfish, the fraudulent and the unimaginative. Sensationalism and distortion in the reporting of news is one form of this abuse. There are many newspapers and magazines that deliberately cater to readers of low intelligence, and by pandering to lax tastes, deprave them further. They are concerned less with the relative importance of events than with their readers' appetite for sensation and their aversion to mental effort. The discovery of a nude body in a river is much more newsworthy — that is, much more appealing to the sluggish mind — than the events that will be the history of the time, or the cultural achievements that will speak for us a thousand years from now. Were we really at such pains to read, that we might read today the sordid details of how a man at the far end of the country murdered his wife, and tomorrow how a countess contrived her divorce, and again the day after how a film star has been arrested for driving whilst drunk?

The same abuse of the privilege of education is apparent in the quality of our television programs, in the petty intrigues of our politicians, in the cut-throat blandishments of unbridled commerce. But it manifests itself above all in the flood of magazines that seem aimed at an audience of morons, and in books of calculated mediocrity that are an indictment of the educational system that produced their authors. It would be reasonable to expect that universal education would enhance the general standard of literary taste, but it seems that the reverse is true. We have taught the whole population to read, but we have not carried their education far enough, or have not educated them in the right way, to develop their tastes or to awaken in them a desire to pursue further what has been begun. The first and only purpose of education should be to awaken a hunger for learning that will demand its own satisfaction.

Thus literacy without true education has created a demand for mediocrity which there are writers and publishers only too eager to satisfy. Since mass demand dictates the economics of literary production, popularity instead of excellence has become the criterion. The highest rewards go to those that please the most people, or that persuade the most people they are being pleased, and in consequence literary standards are continually debased.

Literacy was once the possession of those that prized it most. It went hand in hand with learning and taste, because its accomplishment demanded voluntary effort, and the only motive force was the desire within. Only those read who wanted the best, who were prepared to make whatever mental effort the best demanded. Only those wrote who were worthy of so discriminating an audience.

Perhaps the current situation was inevitable, but one reason it has persisted so long and become so bad is that the true purpose of education has been lost sight of. We no longer educate students to make accessible to them the cultural riches of the world or to set them on the road to the high adventure of learning. Instead, we deliberately trammel their minds, and train them like circus animals to ensure their conformity with the narrow norms of society and to prepare them for their "careers."

Perhaps we shall see in time the dangers of thus narrowing and distorting education and as a result of our enlightenment the popular taste will become more and more discriminating, until there is no longer a place in this world for the charlatans of the pen, the abusers of literature and the debasers of talent for the sake of profit. But by then, how much will have been lost, how irrevocably will the history of the world have been altered, and how many people will have been defrauded of their destiny?

Poets' Pessimism

Modern literature, and modern poetry in particular, is often condemned for its pessimism, but I have never felt that this is the apt word to define the unhappiness that pervades so much of what is being written today.

Pessimism implies a conscious choice of attitude, a deliberate rejection of the hopeful view in favour of the bleak. Contemporary writers in the main have not made such a choice. They have responded to their situation, to the society in which they find themselves, and their response is not one of optimism: but they have not entered into a conspiracy of pessimism and presented a view of life that is distorted by their own joylessness.

It is reasonable to suppose that there is as fair a balance of optimists and pessimists among poets as elsewhere, and the only conclusion to be drawn from the sombre tone of their work is that, even after due allowance has been made for the broadest spectrum of temperament, something remains to disquiet them. In the present state or the present direction of human evolution there must be some ingredient from which even the most extravagantly cheerful of them can distil little hope. And if this is so, it is no more logical to condemn them for darkly reflecting life than to blame the meteorologists for bad weather.

Even if we concede that our literature is pessimistic, is pessimism of this sort necessarily always a bad thing? There is a narrow line indeed between optimism and complacency, and unjustified optimism that obscures the need for remedy can be more poisonous in the body politic than the sourest pessimism.

Possibly the source of this unease — this disease, if one may give the word its archaic as well as its modern meaning — is the gradual erosion by social and material change of the values by which art is sustained, and which it in turn sustains.

The artist needs to believe in the importance of the individual, in the existence of something solid and significant to which all else is relative, and in life itself as a purposeful experience. We all need the assurance of these beliefs for our sanity and stability, and most of our social troubles stem from the faltering of this assurance.

We are all at some time assailed by a sense of the futility of our endeavours, but artists are especially prone to such doubt, and are sometimes destroyed by it, even in a stable society. How much more difficult, then, for them to work with confidence and zest when they cannot have confidence in the life out of which their work must grow. Some critics imply that the poet should extol the marvels of our material progress, should "sing it", in Whitman's sense. Poets have a duty, it is suggested, to be the spokesmen and interpreters of science to the common man. Instead of dwelling on what is being destroyed and protesting the emptiness of what is being created, they should help us to adjust to artificiality and the negation of our true selves.

No true artist is capable of this sort of treachery. He may be awed by the power or complexity of some man-begotten thing, and his awe may move him to creation, but he will not claim that the thing itself is its own justification or that power and complexity are virtues. He is not likely to believe that a machine is better because it can move a mountain in one day instead of two, or leaps to Venus instead of to Mars, unless he is satisfied that some fundamental human need is served thereby: some need not of an imaginary and soulless entity such as the state, or society, or humanity, but of men and women as separate beings whose separateness is precious.

To this concept of the importance of the individual we all pay lip service, but we have little awareness of what it implies or what it demands of us. What is of first importance is not a person's comfort, or welfare, or security, but that person's need and right to be different. Any development that deprives us of this right or obscures our awareness of this need is evil, though it appear to shower us with benefits or steep us in luxury.

The poet is intuitively aware that the meaning of life diminishes as character subsides to a common level, as people conform more and more to pattern. Our general recognition of this was demonstrated by the extravagant veneration in which we held Dr. Albert Schweitzer. It is certainly no detraction from the Doctor's stature to suggest that our admiration was as much for his inspired individuality, for his courage to be himself, as for the philanthropic manner in which he gave it expression.

The other needs, for a solid foundation to which the self can anchor, and for meaning in life, are satisfied less and less with the ever-accelerating pace of change. Man feels himself increasingly enslaved by forces which he himself has created, and over which he has ever less and less control.

He has at times — though perhaps not often enough or strongly enough — the sense of being a prisoner in society, of being fettered by convention. Is there any wonder that this feeling manifests itself in such poems as Al Purdy's "The Machines":

>   ...he managed to retain all 10
> clever fingers and perhaps a soul
> At the end all the submissive
> hymning roar of machines praised him
> for what he was
>   took him for master and lord
> mechanic of their metal destiny until
> one afternoon he shoved a pipe wrench
> into closing jaws and heard them groan
> out steel blood and shriek once
> for their anthropomorhic god
>   Fired
> he went into the street laughing
> picked up a woman near Main & Hastings
> paid her $5 and went to bed and sobbed himself
> to sleep...

Perhaps after all the poets' fault is not that they are pessimistic, but that they are too passively so; that they have not been pessimistic enough, or have not been militant enough in their pessimism, and have not thundered out their dire warnings like the prophets of old.

Poetic Injustice

Russian Poet Andrei Vosnesensky said in a television interview in the United States that the tradition of public recitation, always strong in his country, is still spreading and gathering strength. Now, it is not uncommon for poets to read their work before audiences of 14,000 in sports stadiums.

Soon after the interview with Vosnesensky, Raymond Souster, one of Canada's better known and more prolific poets, reading at Carleton University, also was gratified to find his audience increased since a previous visit. It numbered several dozen. Making allowances for the difference in population between Moscow and Ottawa, one could still wax indignant at the discrepancy.

Two days later the people of Ottawa, who could not be troubled to drive to Carleton to hear Mr. Souster, although he had driven from Toronto to be heard, registered a record attendance of more than 123,000 at the Central Canada Exhibition.

While no poet — least of all Ray Souster — aspires to become a literary Billy Graham, one cannot avoid the conclusion that in the capital city of a country so self-conscious about its culture, such a meagre response to a recent winner of the Governor General's Award for poetry is an indication of something seriously wrong. It is futile to speculate whether the difference in the size of audiences here and in the Soviet Union is related to the stature of the poets or to the temper of the people, for these two are as interdependent as supply and demand in the national economy. If it is true that we have no Voznesensky, no Pasternak — that we have had no Pushkin, no Lermontov — it is equally true that we shall not get them until we deserve them.

It may well be argued that for such occasions as this the publicity is inadequate. Doubtless this is true. But it must be remembered that in a cultural enterprise where money is not available for advertising of the sort that inflates the spurious reputations of those in "show business", publicity is but a reflection of the popular awareness. Word gets around. The occasion becomes news. No serious attempt is made to "sell" poetry, I have heard it said by persons with the beginnings of a promotional gleam in their eye: persons who could not possibly be aware that "sell" is a word with ominous echoes, and that to sell poetry in the one sense would be to sell it inevitably in the other. I am not aware that Tagore had need of a publicity agent to bring flocking to his feet the peasants of India whose illiteracy we donate our dollars to alleviate, or so to establish his hold upon their imagination that his death was mourned — truly and personally mourned — by millions.

It is not without irony after what I have just said, to remember these remarks of Mr. Voznesensky : "So this tradition (of largely-attended public readings) is spreading. My friends and I in Russia have to some extent widened the scope of poetry in this way. But I would like to say...that now our task is to narrow it down and make it more profound."

"Make it more difficult and for smaller audiences?" asked Robert Lowell. To which Voznesensky replied, "Yes." But we should be foolish indeed to take heart from this. A popularized as apart from a popular poetry may well dream of a new depth and exclusiveness, but the smallness of Canadian audiences bears no relation to these things, unless it be to the depth of our darkness and the exclusiveness of our unconcern. Before we can become exclusive we must become inclusive. Or, as Irving Layton said at a reading of his work in 1962 to "as mixed an audience as has been seen since Klondike": "This sort of thing takes poetry out of the classroom and into the marketplace."

After this tirade, I hear you asking, was Raymond Souster really worth going to hear? Certainly it must be confessed that as a declaimer he is no Dylan Thomas, but his poetry does not call for that sort of fiery utterance. Neither the poetry nor the voice that read it was thunderous. He is a quiet man and his work is quiet. So was Tagore's. The quietness of both is deceptive, for with a soft incisive word he can at his best outdo all the trumpets of Jericho. His poetry is of the people — that is to say, accessible to the people — in a way that even Layton's can never be; for, like the common man he is

>   Well-hooked on the past,
>   A sucker for memories.

Souster's simplicity is of the sort, however, that demands concentration. It is the simplicity that comes not from shallow imagery but from the rightness and inevitability born of perfect assimilation of experience.

Yes, it was well worthwhile.

The Privilege of Ignorance

A critic recently confessed himself in danger of falling prey to a phenomenon which he called, half jocularly, "Writer's illiteracy."

There are several reasons for this strange and paradoxical malady, but the chief of them is that writing, if it is worth anything, takes far more time than is commonly imagined. If a man is to be a dedicated writer he has to be prepared to limit his dedication to other pursuits, including reading. Especially, in fact, reading. Invariably he is a man who read much in his youth. From this avidity sprang that love affair with words, the depth and nature of which only other writers can appreciate. It is the essence and the motive power of his urge to write.

A habit acquired so young and so zealously indulged is not easy to control. But the danger of what he writes being unduly coloured by what he reads, before that reading has become truly a part of himself, together with the danger of being seduced from the course of his own industry by the siren-songs of other writers' pens, very soon becomes apparent to him. Writing is first with him, and the measure of his success will depend upon the determination with which he maintains that priority: success being of course understood to be a moral rather than a material thing.

But as his writing grows more and his reading less, he begins to find that he is expected to have some sort of magical awareness of what everyone else has written. His confession that he has read nothing of Moravia or Iris Murdoch is met with raised eyebrows. That he has not yet read the latest Margaret Atwood is an enormity he dare hardly admit to. Who should know all about books, if not a writer? As if writing were like plumbing: a trade learned and practised in common by all, instead of a unique personal endeavour pursued in common by no two.

The problem of the writer, however, is merely a more acute form of a general difficulty. One cannot remain long in a library or bookstore without being overawed by the immensity of knowledge and the limits both of our capacity for it and of the time vouchsafed to us to acquire it.

Of course this limitation is not confined to books. We read more and more often of the burden of knowledge being imposed upon modern man. This seems to assume that we must all have the same knowledge, that we must conform in what we know, as in all else. I protest. Every man is entitled to the privilege of ignorance. Indeed, it is one of his most important privileges, and it becomes more vital to his sanity — and to the world's — as the scope of knowledge broadens.

We are shaped as much by our ignorance as by our knowledge, for we are individual not to the extent of what we have in common with others, but to the extent that we differ. It is how we exercise our privilege of ignorance that makes us what we are. We must select what we will know, and how we shall apply that knowledge. To be fully and fruitfully what we are, we must be allowed the privilege of not being what we are not. In an age that brings to bear ever-increasing pressures of conformity, it becomes perhaps the most precious of our freedoms.

Society must demand certain conformities, but it will be a strong and viable society only to the extent that it is a complex of widely various individuals. It will be weakened, not enriched, by the levelling out of differences. To the extent that a man yields to the pressure to acquire knowledge, or to meet demands beyond those of his own individuality, beyond his own special calling to fulfill himself, to that extent he is less a poet, less a physicist, less a farmer. We are all diminished by the need to know how to compute our income tax, for this pressure to know is a tax upon our selfhood.

Perhaps it is time we re-examined the whole of our philosophy of education from this standpoint. We learn with increasing frequency of students being driven to the point of breakdown by the pressure upon them to absorb an ever-broadening range of knowledge. This is a symptom of fundamental failure, for despite the breadth of the curriculum and the refinements in the technique of teaching, the primary aim of education is obviously not being met if students are not learning how to be confidently and harmoniously themselves.

The Age of Impatience

One lesson the arts are capable of teaching in this, the Impatient Century, is that there are some things worth taking a little time over; things that can and must be taken at the same leisurely pace and with the same thorough commitment that they demanded of our grandparents. For it is characteristic of all true art that it will not be hurried, either in its execution or in its appreciation. Not that, in our passion for instant this and instant that, attempts have not been made to defy the time-demands of art, to force it into conformity with the headlong acceleration of material "progress." Since we tend to regard speed as a virtue in itself, rather than as a mere convenience — and often a dubious convenience at that — it is natural that we should try to carry it over from our material into our cultural and spiritual life. These attempts have resulted in such phenomena as accidental painting, where colours are thrown or splashed or in some other random manner conveyed to the canvas without involving the "artist" in the agony of decision. This is obviously a great advantage, for it is this tiresome business of conscious application that takes all the time. By freeing himself of the foolish notion of form, by shrugging off the enormous vanity of imagining that he can order things better than God, the artist removes the obstacles to instant art and opens the way for his function to be taken over by machines. What folly, after all, to imagine that one way of putting colours on canvas is better than another.

In the same category, perhaps, have been the attempts to compose poetry and music by computers, although these seem to have been prompted more by idle curiosity than by serious motive. All these are fatuous and may be ignored because they are the work of cranks and idle dabblers. They neglect the simple fact that the validity of any form of art stems from its growth out of the life and experience of a human being, and its value is proportional to the intensity with which that experience infuses it. Unless we accept this as a first principle, any child with a kaleidoscope becomes peer to the most exalted artistic genius.

In literature, the attempts to speed up the process of appreciation take two forms. One is to increase the rate at which the brain devours words. The other, which has a similar result, is to reduce the number of words by producing a condensation or digest. Both methods seem to presuppose that the purpose of reading a book is to get to the end of it in the shortest possible time rather than to reap the maximum reward in appreciation.

A radio announcer a few days ago terminated an advertisement for a speed-reading course by commenting: "You'll be able to read the average novel in twenty minutes." I am well aware that this was jocular, but the seed of belief was there, and no doubt lies germinal in more than one credulous ear.

No one would deny that there is a place for rapid reading, but that place is not in the enjoyment of literature. There are times when it is desirable to acquire much information in a short time, but one does not become learned or wise simply by gorging books, any more than one attains health by bolting inordinate amounts of food: one does well to digest well a moderate, well-chosen quantity of each.

Speeding through a book is like speeding across country. One covers the ground and can claim to have made the trip, but arrives at one's destination, if the end of a book may be called a destination, with but a blurred and superficial impression of the territory. For me, reaching the end of a good book is more like parting from an old friend. But reading is like travel in this, that it is what one does on the journey that broadens the mind, not the distance covered nor the despatch with which one covers it.

It seems less than courteous to toss off in half an hour a book to which a writer of acknowledged genius has given his deepest thought and feeling for two or three years, but it is not this disproportion in time that is important. Who would not work thus to provide a fleeting but recurrent pleasure for the generations to come? What is important is whether we can really imbibe what a book has to offer if we zip through it in half an hour, instead of letting it fill our leisure and pervade our consciousness for several days.

Both in creation and in appreciation there is a time dimension. It is not a matter of mechanics but a matter of feeling, of savouring, of exposure to it as to the sun. The time lapse is intrinsic to it, is a part of the pleasure. There is no more to be gained by compressing it than by playing the record of a symphony at double speed. And what, after all, is the hurry? Why are we at such great pains to finish one book so that we may start another? To save time? For what? Speed is justifiable only if the time saved is put to better use. And what better use is there?

Flowers and Evil

Every crisis in the march of humanity leaves some sort of record on the walls of the cave of time. After man's degradation in the war years it is not surprising that we should get novels like *Dog Years*, plays like *The Deputy*, films like *The Pawnbroker*. It would be distressing if we did not. The time has come for them. For, as a Saturday Review writer pointed out, "All serious writing... is a distilling of essences from the mash of experience."

Nevertheless there are several dubious assumptions. One is that men in general are crazed with guilt. Another is that the excising of guilt is in itself sufficient reason and stimulus for the creation of a work of art. A third is that the mere reiteration of shameful events can, by appeal to our moral sense alone, cast out the evils those events expressed or engendered. To portray evil without compassion is merely to multiply it.

Irving Layton in one of his admirable ringing prefaces deplored that poetry had not, like the novel and the drama, come to grips with this universal evil and guilt. "Today, poets must teach themselves to imagine the worst...They must have the severity to descend from one level of foulness to another and learn ... there is no bottom, no end." He speaks of "...terrible meanings embedded in the human ash of death factories," and asks, "Where is the poet who can make clear for us Belsen? Vorkuta? Hiroshima?"

No one would deny that it is desirable and pressing that some poets should do this, but to insist that they all must, and to condemn en masse all the poets of our generation because they have not, is impertinence and even stupidity in Mr. Layton. It would only be necessary to quote from his own work, much of which I greatly admire, to demonstrate that he knows it.

It is legitimate and necessary to ask where the poets are who should have written of these things, but not to revile those that have written of other things. Should we condemn our dentist because he allows people to die — perhaps dies himself — of cancer? Should we not rather be thankful that he cures our toothache?

Inevitably literature must reflect concern for the depth of human degradation, and perhaps through the subtle workings of compassion it may effect that desired heightening of moral sensibility. But it must reflect the whole of life, display the complete spectrum of human nature, from the ultra-violet of man's basest evil to the infra-red of his highest nobility.

There must be concern with evil, but what Mr. Layton advocates is obsession, and obsession with evil would be worse than evil itself. If Mr. Layton has such an obsession it is evidently not operative all the time. Was he thinking of Belsen when he wrote that his mind was balanced upon the buttocks of his beloved? Or when he wrote that tender poem to his daughter? Yet he writes contemptuously of Yeats, Eliot and Pound, and says their work is "hardly to the point in an age of mass terror, mass degradation, when the human being has less value than a bedbug or cockroach."

One basic fallacy in all this is that evil is a matter of magnitude rather than of intensity. Vileness and cruelty have always existed, and although massacre is more foul and terrifying it is difficult to believe that a pious inquisitor watching one young girl burning at the stake was any nearer heaven than an Eichmann decreeing the death of thousands.

Balance is necessary in all things. We should not shrink from the study of man's vileness, but it would be folly to demand that every writer whip himself into a frenzy of remorse before taking up the pen. Cleanliness, sanity and wisdom are not attainable through the unremitting contemplation of filth. We must celebrate the glory and hope of the life remaining, as well as the horror and despair of the death that has descended.

Let us not insist that all persons with a vision of beauty and a talent for its expression shut their eyes upon that vision. If there comes a new Keats, let us not condemn him to cry death in the marketplace, or if another Cellini, let us demand of him something other than urns for the ashes of civilization.

Society and Solitude

We hear it said with growing frequency and with ingenious variations that writing is a lonely occupation. This is so evidently true that the compulsion to reiterate it is probably symptomatic of something. The reiteration itself is not harmful. This is a truth we need to be constantly reminded of: but what perturbs is that these words are uttered so often in a tone of querulous complaint, as if to be alone were one of life's major calamities.

With the writer, this reluctance to be alone stems from his awareness that once alone he must take up the pitifully small sword of his talent and go forth feeling overwhelmed and inadequate upon the battlefield of his own mind, where there are dragons to be slain if he will but have faith. But faith is a fickle ally. He will back you up bravely against fearful odds, slay monsters, work miracles of prowess and let you take the credit: but once look over your shoulder to reassure yourself that he is there and he will turn tail, cringe like the meanest cur and abandon you to the hordes of the enemy.

The writer, then, has some excuse, and his success in resisting the seductions of this excuse is the measure of his greatness. But this aversion to solitude is not confined to writers. It is a creeping malaise of modern society. It is not necessary to observe our contemporaries very long to discover that they are afraid to be alone. They will go to astonishing lengths to avoid it. They will practise all manner of self-deceptions. They will devise endless activity to keep themselves from noticing that they are avoiding it.

"In solitude," says Byron, "we are at least alone." Under the cynical exterior of this apparent platitude there is abundance of truth. There is recognition that to be alone can be salutary, pleasant, and sometimes necessary; that "solitude sometimes is best society." I believe it is no exaggeration to say that solitude is as beneficent and vital to the flagging spirit as sleep to the weary body. It is grateful and restorative. It enables us to regain our lost perspectives, to test the mass reactions that have beguiled or confused us with the infallible litmus of our own inner being.

However reliant we become on the resources of a complex and interdependent society, we can relate to that society, preserve its sanity and control its destiny, and make it meaningful and noble as the consummation of all that is best in our various individualities, only if we assess it, and our own contribution to it, in the peace of "the soul's calm sunshine." For deep within us lies the unwavering lode of personal conviction, without reference to which all impressions from without are of equal validity, wisdom and sophistry are one. We veer from the true north of our destiny, pursuing the comfortable wake of others; not because their compasses are less infirm than our own, but because they appear to navigate with more assurance.

We are saved from complete aimlessness and endless vacillation only by the prevailing winds of our prejudice. The pen is mightier than the sword, and it will be mightier than the nuclear bomb, simply because those who wield it must court solitude to think, while the "thinking" of the majority in an age of bustle and preoccupation will be, as it so often has been in the past, a mere emotional acceptance of the sophistry of others.

I suspect that modern man is afraid to be alone because he is afraid to think; not only because he fears what he may see if he withdraws his head from the sands of convention and dogma, but because he has grown averse to the very process of thought. His mind shies from it, procrastinates with regard to it, just as his obese and indolent body shirks from day to day the exercise it needs for its health. It is more comfortable to follow a quack diet, to submit to mass thinking, to follow the prevailing mode of belief. Fashion, once confined to such vanities as dress, now invades every sphere of human activity. In an age whose most urgent need is for people of vision to lead, we make a virtue of following.

There is somewhere a great mistake, for solitude offers pleasures and many rewards. The wise of the ages have testified to it. The poets in their highest moments extol it, grow lyrical over "That inward eye that is the bliss of solitude." They make bold to suggest that:

> One self-approving hour whole years outweighs
> Of stupid starers and of loud huzzas:
> And more true joy Marcellus exiled feels
> Than Caesar with a senate at his heels.

And this is a pleasure we should learn to value more as the opportunity to enjoy it grows less, as life's complexity augments and each person's privacy diminishes.

The most terrifying thing about the vast uncontrolled upsurge of population is not the threat of starvation (physical starvation, that is), for our materialistic science will take good, if not timely, care of that: it is the threat of overcrowding, the possibility that there will be a time when there is no longer a place where a person may go apart to steep himself in solitude, to discover the joys and strengths of meditation, which is becoming already a lost art, and to acquire the only true knowledge — the knowledge of himself. We prattle much of peace, but there can be no hope of peace among nations until we can learn to be at peace with ourselves.

One of the few encouraging aspects of the current obsession with outer space, upon which we squander so lavishly our resources of money and mind, is the hope it holds out to us that, though the men and women who venture to the far reaches of the universe may find but small reward for their endeavours, may find no life sequestered there in the infinite fields of space, they may at least be forced, in those awful solitudes, to rediscover themselves.

Tolerance

Did literature need any justification beyond its mere pleasurable existence, it would surely be that it teaches us tolerance. And if our age is to be remembered at all, it must be as the Age of Tolerance: not because we are more largely endowed than other ages with that virtue, but because there may be none to remember us unless we somehow speedily acquire it.

A problem more pressing by far than the shortage of scientists, over which we so urgently concern ourselves, is the dearth of tolerant men; for the complex and costly machinery of modern education grinds out a spate of scientific genius in vain if it produce also men who mistrust one another.

It is good that there should be specialists, that every man should work the soil most fertile to his talent, and life is infinitely enriched by men's diversity. But it is a strange paradox that although we have a militant fear of compulsion to a grey and regimented uniformity, we cannot tolerate in others the things that make them different from ourselves. We have also a way of assuming that if two things are different, one of them must be wrong or inferior; and since each man stands at the centre of his own world, it is not surprising that he tends to regard everything alien to his own experience as wrong, everyone beyond his narrow horizon as foreign, and every idea perverse or worthless that does not accord with his own. The more remote these things are from his own smug centre, the greater will be his hostility and suspicion.

If he is a man of small consequence he will band together with others of like stature to secure himself against the strange, to armour himself against the unexpected and fortify himself with comfortable conventions. He heartily embraces all that conforms to the reassuring pattern into which he has fitted himself, and since he is an enlightened being he "tolerates" all else. But tolerance is a two-edged word, like charity. There are two kinds of tolerance, and in time we learn to practise the one and eschew the other. There is the insulting tolerance of grudging condescension, and the true and generous tolerance of acceptance and desire to understand. True tolerance calls for insight, not indulgence; for an awareness that all our differences make us but complementary parts of a whole, and that our diversities derive their true value from our being, beneath it all, fundamentally the same.

The secret of tolerance is knowledge. Intolerance is born of fear; fear, of ignorance. Charles Lamb in his jocular wisdom said, "How could I hate anyone I know?" It does well to ponder this question. The answer would disband armies, stay the hand of violence, curb the tongue of malice.

To know. But how does one come by this sort of knowledge, this intuitive placing of oneself in alien shoes? How contrive not merely to accept, to forgive, even to love another's difference from us, but to be in spirit different with him?

When we say that art and literature deal in universal truths, we mean simply that they are capable of imparting this knowledge from one to another. Understanding and accepting each other's differences must begin from that inner core of humanity wherein we are all the same. At this perceptive centre, around which our peculiarities have accreted through the accidents of birth, upbringing and random event, we are each potentially all other human beings: the sinner a saint, the white man black, the weak man strong and the strong weak. It is only by summoning forth this potential that we can achieve true understanding, and hence true tolerance.

It is from this perceptive centre also that true literature is produced, and by it that it is recognized. It has often been said that one of the prime attributes of a great writer is compassion; that is, the ability to feel with others. The extent of his greatness will be the extent to which he is free of the hard shell of prejudice that is ever ready to calcify and thicken about man's sensitive, compassionate core.

The writer who cannot orient himself to the viewpoint, cannot occupy the very skin, excite to the very heartbeat of another — to another if need be of different creed, or race, or social standing, or even sex — is condemned to write to a drab time-worn formula. His best effort of creation will be plagiarized from imitations of imitations. And such writing, because it is conceived in prejudice, begets prejudice. Because it is not born within that deep core of humanity it cannot aspire to reach it.

Thus it is that some men read much and remain intolerant still. Their reading, like their living, is bound by convention and staled by habit. They read for a lifetime about crime but never reach an understanding of how it feels to be a criminal; or about war without tasting its afflictions; or about race hatred without suspecting what it is to suffer in the alien skin of the hated.

It is for this reason that literature and the arts — not science — must form the basis of any true education. It is only through the appreciation of these things that we come to an appreciation of each other. There has been an increasing tendency for the institutions of learning to confuse training with education. It seems to me that we should train men and women in the exploitation of their differences only after education has taught them the value and the sanctity of what they have in common. Tolerance is born of wisdom, and wisdom has nothing to do with fact or formula. It is generated by that commerce between the hearts of men which enables us to come to an understanding of others by knowledge of ourselves, and of ourselves by knowledge of others.

History and Literature

Aristotle was too rigid and too naive to be the great critic he is sometimes acclaimed. He was too fond of rules. Some of the rules he crystallized from the prevailing currents of his time are a strait-jacket upon the instruction of literature. They have been the bane of writers ever since. The charlatans who undertake to teach the gullible how to write could hardly turn a penny without him. Nevertheless he did sometimes give his instinctive wisdom rein and shed his light rather than his shadow down the centuries: as in his notorious declaration that "poetry is more philosophical and more worthy of serious attention than history; for while poetry is concerned with universal truths, history treats of particular facts."

It is a gambit calculated to shatter the peace of any common-room. One imagines with sympathy the indignation of some mute inglorious Gibbon at finding himself thus weighed in the balance against the metrical Gertrude Steins of our generation and found wanting. But old Aristotle's point is a valid one nevertheless; and it is no less valid because some poets hide their lack of universal (or any other) significance under a bushel of obscurity. Here, it is the stature of the poets, not the stature of their art that is in question. To qualify as poets by Aristotle's yardstick they must concern themselves with universal truths; and here the matter comes clearly into focus, for such truths are not only universal, but timeless. When a poem has survived a thousand years, who will question that it is "more philosophical and more worthy of serious attention" than the history out of which it grew?

But all this does start an interesting speculation. What is — and what should be — the relation between literature and history? Aristotle seems to suggest that they are not compatible, but this is obviously not so and I cannot believe that such was his intention. But he did accentuate their separateness, and it is a false division that has persisted. It is an unfortunate fallacy that impoverishes the one and dessicates the other. How can history be recorded, in any coherent and comprehensible form, apart from literature? For it is not sufficient, whatever Aristotle may have said, merely to register the facts. The historian has just as much responsibility to bring facts to life as the poet has to breathe life into his universal truths. Without this faculty the historian becomes merely an antiquarian, and the poet a moralist.

If a historical work written today is read a century hence it will be not because it is good history but because it is good literature. Much bad history survives and at last triumphs over mere fact by sheer literary merit, by eclipsing with its universal verities the lesser truths of reality. Perhaps to a man who has steeped himself in the study of the past, the ancient events and the forgotten men present themselves in all their dramatic immediacy and colour. What other explanation can there be for so much grubbing and verifying and raising of dust? But this perceptive experience does not become history until it is captured and transmitted in all its depth and intensity. Perhaps the reason there is so much dull history is that the historians experience but cannot communicate, perceive but do not know how to evoke. Perhaps they burn up so much vital energy in creating their own certainty that they have none left to re-create it for others; that is, to effect the necessary fusion between history and literature.

Without such a fusion there can be no meaning to history, any more than there is meaning in saying that a given rock is a million years old without considering what it means to be a million years old, without making some imaginative effort to evoke the surroundings and the very throes of the rock's origin; to glimpse the ebb and flow of life about it while through all those ages it lay inanimate and dumb. Only thus are we suitably awed by antiquity.

I cannot recall that I learned any history at school. I am not even sure that one can learn history, any more than one can learn literature or art. I had a few dates hammered ineradicably into my consciousness, and a few names, and the lifeless titles of a few events: but it was not until, through the alchemy of literature, I had lived at those times, moved among those men and participated in those events that they became significant to me as history. I learned more of history in five rapt minutes in the Bloody Tower than in all those dreary classroom hours that taught me only where a few meaningless events were fixed in an unimaginable scale of time.

It is only because some historians have but half done their job, or perhaps because some writers have not sufficiently aided them in it, that teachers of history are necessary. There would be little justification for teaching what any person might more easily and enjoyably find out for himself. The teachers of history exist only because the historians need interpreters, need someone to dramatize and explain, to wipe away the dust and verdigris from the life that underlies their "particular facts." It is evident that what is needed is not a distinction between history and literature, but a marriage; for if the "particular facts" of history are properly and creatively presented, they become the universal truths of literature.

4

The Turning of Leaves

Mighty Works

I believe it was Thomas Mann who said that a mighty work must have a mighty theme. It seems a valid, perhaps even a transparent assertion, and certainly one would not wish to contest it with that father of mighty works; but it does leave one wondering in what this quality of mightiness consists.

It is, after all, the ingredient we in Canada seem to find hardest to instil into our literature. It is what we expect to find in that ardently-awaited masterwork that shall signal our cultural coming of age; that first truly great book out of which the soul-hunger of this nation has created a need and a legend. We see it standing alone and unmistakable, head and shoulders above all others, a giant work whose stature the most diffident of us cannot deny, nor the most disdainful ignore. It will be mighty.

But how, mighty? Mighty in breadth, like *War and Peace*? Mighty in depth, like *Faust*? Studiously mighty, like Gibbon's *Decline and Fall* or mighty in its simplicity, like *Pilgrim's Progress*? Voluminously mighty like the works of Mann himself or mightily to the point, like Bacon's?

Certainly there are mighty themes. The world abounds in them, and the world's literature abundantly reflects them. Homer, Aeschylus, Shakespeare spring immediately to mind. An ingredient of their greatness seems to have been the perception of the nobly dramatic, of the magnificence in the scope of things that makes events Olympian and men godlike. Possessed of such a theme, we tend in our more naive moments to believe the battle of literary composition is more than half won. Creation becomes, so to speak, a piece of cake. Who, conceived according to Tristram Shandy's theories of genetics, in a moderate literary fervour, could not, given these propitious materials, toss off an *Iliad* or a *Hamlet* in time for the CBC writing competition?

Is it then so difficult to perceive, this mightiness in the doings of men, this fatal magnificence in the march of events? Was Ned Pratt really the only one susceptible to the Homeric stature of Brebeuf, the only one whose eye and heart were open, whose pen ready? And Robert Service, with all his shallowness and crude constraints, was he alone accessible to the grandeur of the northland as a liberator of epic forces in the human heart? For one has to acknowledge that when Service has been critically demolished, a certain rude mightiness remains. He will not be left out of anthologies. For the rest, the more sourly chauvinistic might point to Evangeline and suggest that we allow our resource of mighty themes to be exploited in the same way as every other.

I believe that the truth might be more nearly come at by a travesty of Mann's dictum: a mighty theme must have a mighty work. Or, more precisely still, a mighty worker. There may be a valid distinction between works that are mighty in subject and those that are mighty in execution, but it is a thing of little moment. The crude ore of event, however heroic, must be refined and wrought upon before it is freely accepted into the currency of literature. It demands a mastery and a verve without which it goes dumb in the hearts of the beholders to the grave, or lies fallow down the gossiping generations until its Homer or its Shakespeare comes.

The mightiness, it seems, resides as much in the pen as in the theme. *Hamlet* in lesser hands would have been but a thing of a day, a more sordid and less credible *Peyton Place*. And had not the clamour at the gates of Troy been echoed in the thunder of Homeric verse, the battle that begot the *Iliad* would be deservedly forgotten like a thousand barbaric clashes, no less heroic, before and since. There is no heroism, only admiration. The epic is not in the events but in our response to the events and in their exultant celebration. The bookshelves of the world sag with insipid historical romances whose themes are potentially as mighty as any in literature. Here in Canada the stories of Louis

Riel and other dormant giants of literature have been done to death in a dozen different ways.

Often, indeed, the mightiness is not intrinsic to the subject at all, but is conferred upon it by the creative concern of the author. He generates an epic heat from it by the sheer energy and intensity of his perception, that transforms and ennobles even as it apprehends. Thus Goethe in his *Faust*. Thus Henry James, whose mightiness was microscopic. Thus Thomas Mann, who was able to find a mighty theme in a TB sanitorium. Where there are mighty writers there will always be mighty themes: where there are none, the most glorious events will gather archival dust.

The Turning of Leaves

A Toronto publisher predicts that in a few years the book as we know it today will have gone the way of the warming pan and the antimacassar; it will be collected and gloated over by the acquisitive as a relic of days past, but as a medium of communication in the new environment it will be about as practical as the Dead Sea Scrolls. The smug teenager of tomorrow will snigger at its clumsy inadequacy as now he sniggers at the silent film, as if all the credit for subsequent "improvement" were his own.

The "book" will be an electronic device about the size of a novel. Earlier models will perhaps have the bulk of Tolstoy or Thomas Mann, but research will pare it down to pocket size. Into this reproducing device will fit minute cartridges containing the text of the volume we wish to read. This text will be projected on a screen forming the front of the device, a page at a time, and the page will be "turned" by pressing a button.

Now all this is extremely logical and utilitarian. Perhaps in our enslaved age of gadgetry it is inevitable. Yet it seems to reactionary, stick-in-the-mud me, who believes that man should be served rather than enslaved by his machines, that there is some monstrous misconception here; some blindness to the complexity of the reading experience. Efficiency has its place, of course, in reading as in anything else. When the sole purpose of the reader is to acquire information, automation will and perhaps should have its way: but this is something quite apart from the enjoyment of literature, and it seems no more reasonable to me to mechanize this process than to attempt to speed-read Shakespeare.

One has to admit that human values change, and that a society that puts plastic flowers on graves is capable of accepting mechanical books; but the person that accepts either is likely to be no more aware of the aesthetic experience of reading than of the wonder that is a flower. If utility were the one end of all things, most of life's meaning would vanish. Why should we drink from fragile, beautifully wrought glass by candlelight, when a plastic mug under a brash fluorescence would serve as well?

It is necessary to examine one's responses very carefully in matters of this sort. Is it perhaps mere nostalgia? A mellowing man's tendency to form habits and resist change? I have thought very carefully upon it: and the more evident it becomes to me that the textbook, the reference work and perhaps even the newspaper of tomorrow will become in some manner automated, the more a rebellious inmost part of me insists that it must not happen to the books we read for pleasure. It must not happen because the book itself, for all its clumsy bulk, its dust-gathering propensity and its inefficiency as an instrument of communication, contributes to and in a very marked degree conditions the pleasure of reading it.

The sight and feel of a book, though it be the most disreputable dog-eared paperback in the world, are important ingredients in its enjoyment: to have the thing in one's hands entire; to augment through the sentient fingertips the impressions of the eager eye; to turn a page and pause in meditation, a finger upon the author's pulse — in this very act of turning a page there is a subtle pleasure and a deep symbolism, a sense of adventure and renewal and regenerate hope. The fact that the words were on a screen, however page-like the screen might be, would somehow place an obstruction between the author and the reader, would diminish or destroy that vital sympathy between them. The printed word on a television or cinema screen is annoying and seldom effective because it cannot achieve this rapport, this essential intimacy; and the same is true of writing that appears anywhere other than on a page. It informs but it does not involve us. "Books that you may carry to the fire, and hold readily in your hand," observed Dr. Johnson, "are the most useful after all." And not only the most useful, but the most enjoyable. The tome in the reference library, which one must approach to read *in situ* as though it were a tombstone, seldom engages more than the dry intellectual husk of our spirit.

Observe the man in the bus, how his fingers caress the tattered volume he pries loose from his pocket, how his eyes glaze and glow and course across the page as though the words were racehorses, how from time to time his lips involuntarily stir to the rhythm of the words like feet impatient to dance; and how he inserts now and then a meditative forefinger between the pages while he gazes off into some far and glowing distance, oblivious to clatter and jolt and stink of gasoline, coming to terms with truth. But observe again his neighbour, whose eyes range over the advertisements around him with a dull and terrible apathy, or shy away from the words as though ashamed to be caught at it. Though the very word of God be emblazoned there — as sometimes indeed it is — it will kindle neither his heart nor his imagination. He cannot take it in his hands and make it intimately his.

Books, collectively, also make their impact. In a library the very assemblage of books operates benignly upon the spirit. There is a climate of literature that wraps one about, soothes away our preoccupations with the world's futilities, and infuses us with wisdom and peace by a sort of spiritual osmosis. It is for the maintenance of this climate, rather than for the convenience of those that wish to read (your true reader will read in Bedlam itself) that we are enjoined to silence. We imbibe literature through our very pores, and I sometimes have the droll fancy that the unlettered might attain to wisdom simply by sitting long hours in a library and exposing themselves to the subtle emanations, to the spiritual radiance of books.

The Alice Phenomenon

It is extremely improbable that when Charles Lutwidge Dodgson published *Alice's Adventures in Wonderland* in July 1865, his lively imagination conceived the possibility of the event's being commemorated with such enthusiasm now, one hundred years later, in a country that at that time was still in turbulent gestation in the womb of the New World.

He was a lecturer in mathematics at Oxford, but he would not have considered good enough to be worth computing the odds on his tale becoming, as it has, a sort of common denominator of literacy throughout the English-speaking world. He could hardly have foreseen that Alice would be quoted more than Hamlet, and usually to better effect. When his learned colleagues ribbed him — as no doubt they did, unmercifully — about the nature of his literary accomplishment, neither he nor they could be expected to believe that some of the greatest men of the ensuing century would unashamedly use the words of Alice to lend cogency and point to their own wisdom (and lesser men to disguise their lack of it).

Yet all this, and much more, the tale has achieved, and it may profit us to inquire why. How is it that the children of today — monsters though we may sometimes insist they are — are still attracted and delighted by Alice in defiance of all the seductions of film, television and Beatles that would draw them away from books, and all the attempts of extravagant lithography and addictive "science" to win them back again to books of another and lesser sort? And why do we children of yesterday, hard pressed as we now are by the legions of fact and stern reality, still seem to draw light and a subtle, strengthening faith from this fantasy?

One of the reasons for this miraculous survival and this profound influence is no doubt that the book's creation engaged the whole person of its author, and in consequence engages the whole person of the reader. It was not done by a part of the writer that wanted to make money, or achieve fame, or instruct the young, or advance a cause, or pursue any other good but insufficient end. It was the gift of himself entire, prompted perhaps by the eager surrender of the three young listeners as they glided that July afternoon down the sun-dappled river. Only thus is the highest and happiest expression achieved, by an unstinting gift of this sort, a free and generous outflowing of the writer's talent for simple joy that exists in him and will out, on its own untrammelled terms.

But the heart of the secret lies in the fantasy itself, for despite the wry pronouncements of Dr. Brock Chisholm to the contrary, the imaginative experiences of childhood are far more important than the mere acquisition of knowledge. Truths that are apprehended through the tingling certitudes of fantasy in youth — and many are the truths, dear Doctor, that are accessible in no other way, though it is too late in life for you to discover it — glow comfortably in the heart of a man and arm him for his little heroisms, spur him to his little triumphant miracles when computers and common sense proclaim him licked before he starts.

Stimulation and exercise of the imagination in the young sets free a great dynamic force, and begets men unafraid of their own imaginative potential. Fantasy is not an escape into unreality, but a reduction of reality to its essence, an extraction of the universal and timeless from the dross of the immediate. Facts and observations are the crudest ore. It is not until they have been refined in the slow fires of thought, and wrought upon with love by a creator, that they become the heirlooms of civilization.

The triumph of Alice is that, while its simple wisdom and satire illuminate its own and any age, it succeeds in shaking itself entirely free of contemporary concerns to speak to its readers of universal things in a way they can not only understand but enjoy. It speaks to them as equals because on that happy afternoon the three girls and their friend were equals, and any assumption of superiority, any hint of condescension would have destroyed immediately the rapt attention by which the listeners were able to pursue —

> The dream-child moving through a land
> Of wonders wild and new,
> In friendly chat with bird or beast —
> And half believe it true.

How different are so many of the books we contemptuously term "juveniles" today, whose fantasies fail miserably because they are patronizing and tongue-in-cheek, and whose practicalities tether the hungry minds of childhood to the scrub pastures of sordid reality. We have become obsessed with the need to "prepare the young reader for life," and in our preoccupation with this necessity we destroy all hope of meeting it. "But there is so much they must know nowadays," we say, and proceed to stuff them so full of facts about the material things of today and tomorrow that the very spirit of youth must vomit. They will have their fill of the wonders of science and the catalogue of man's clevernesses "ere the voice of dread" shall summon them, wondering bitterly what life was all about, "to unwelcome bed."

The same fallacy is abroad in education, which occupies itself a great deal with the practical need to make a living, but very little with the spiritual need to make a life. "A student," it has been profoundly observed, " is not a vessel to be filled but a lamp to be lighted." And so is a young reader. Alice has lighted more lamps, prepared more young people for life — and enriched and strengthened them in it — than all the tomes of philosophy, all the wide-eyed looks at modern marvels, and all the lavishly illustrated inanities in ten ponderous volumes. For the authors and advocates of these books — all valuable and desirable in their place, but lethal to the spirit out of it — have not learned that he who never spoke to a flower will never know what a flower knows, and will never, in the matters that make life truly meaningful, be able to speak to anybody.

Fact and Fiction

We cannot but deplore the decline in the popularity of fiction, yet the ill wind of materialism that brings about this decline is not without its burden of comfort for those to whom the health of literature is a matter of concern. For although it is a social disgrace that the author of a culturally significant novel in Canada usually does not earn enough in royalties to pay his rent for the time it takes to write it, the effect of this has been to discourage those for whom the writing of fiction was a business rather than an art, a matter of personal profit rather than of personal satisfaction.

The compulsive writers, the writers who have a creative turbulence to get out of their systems and find in the novel the only satisfactory way of doing it, continue stubbornly to write fiction in defiance of all the dire warnings of the academics, and despite the blandishments of some publishers who are shortsighted enough to believe that writers should follow, rather than create, the demand.

Is it too much to hope that what will disappear will be the "pot-boiler", the popular, formula-written novel that comes from the assembly line of its author's brain with clockwork precision every year in time for the publisher's fall list? Already much less in evidence are the short stories of the same low calibre that used to crowd the pages of magazines and weekly newspapers, which were a source of steady income for the dabblers and hacks who assembled them like plastic model kits to blueprints supplied by so-called schools of writing. Stories of this type are now almost exclusively confined to those women's magazines that have slept through the revolt of women against the image those magazines project, where they can do little harm.

The serious short story now finds publication in the high quality literary magazines, in the "little" magazines and in occasional volumes from publishers with a sense of responsibility for the nation's literature. Only the first of these outlets offers writers fair payment for their work, but the standard demanded by all three is usually very high. Today the short story writer must be capable of producing work of a quality that will win the high stakes offered by such magazines as *Atlantic Monthly*, or must have sufficient belief in the short story as a viable art form to be prepared to write virtually for nothing. A few valiant souls will doubtless keep the art of fiction alive until a climate more favourable to it again prevails.

The decline in the demand for fiction has resulted from our preoccupation with factual knowledge. There is a tendency to regard fiction as something utterly divorced from the realities of life, and therefore unworthy of our attention in a scientific age. There is so much to be learned about the material environment we have made for ourselves that there is no time for make-believe. Why read of imaginary adventures when one can read — as well as see and hear — the real-life adventures of astronauts, explorers, deep-sea divers, mountaineers?

In the first place, of course, these adventures do not become real for us until they have been dramatized: until they have, in effect, been turned into fiction. Communication of experience requires more than the mere passing of information from one person to another. Nothing could be more pointless than those interviews we are so often subjected to, in which the inarticulate try so painfully to give spontaneous expression to some exciting or unusual experience.

Fiction is not an escape from reality but a means of reaching a higher understanding of it. The aim of the novelist is not to invent something that does not exist, but to shed upon the reality around him a reflected light from fictional experience. A make-believe is merely a device for arriving more directly and more precisely at what is true. The story is in many cases a comparatively small and unimportant ingredient of a novel, no more an end in itself than a mirror is. We do not look at a mirror, we look into it at what it shows us of ourselves. Without it we tend to have a grossly distorted idea of what we are really like. Through ignorance of ourselves we become vain and intolerant of others.

Fiction appeals to all our other selves and makes available to us all their intuitive wisdom, all their emotional resources. The existence of these dormant identities in us explains the phenomenon of the human love of make-believe, of man's instinctive recognition of the need for and the great potency of fiction. It explains why, in spite of the materialists' contempt for fiction as "mere fairy tales," some of the world's greatest minds have been devoted to the creation of it, and why others of comparable intellect have read it and have been enriched by it.

That we may become unresponsive to this need is one of the great perils of our materialistic age. In our attempts to reconcile the diverse influences abroad in the world we need the deep insights of the novelist, the short story writer and the dramatist more than ever. Our challenge lies not in the scientific isolation of the truth, which in most cases requires only persistence, but in the toleration of what our own narrowness of vision makes error, which demands all the strength and nobility of our deepest humanity.

Satisfactions of the Pen

If you ask professional writers why they write (and I use the word professional to indicate the measure of dedication rather than the size of income), the lucidity of their replies will be in inverse proportion to their accomplishment. At the lower end of the scale will be the smug extrovert who says, "For the money, what else?" The conviction is absolute, and all who profess otherwise are hypocrites.

On the pinnacle are the literary geniuses, who will starve before they will abandon what they feel themselves destined to do, yet are nonplussed at the need to tell you why. They will take refuge in metaphor or in fluid generalities, but usually you can manoeuvre them into a position where they will admit that they write because they want to; or rather, because they have to. To starve physically is less harrowing than to starve spiritually.

What, then, are the satisfactions of the pen? Is there any affinity of motive between a Shakespeare and a Spillane; between the monumental failure of James Joyce's *Ulysses* and the pathetic triumph, once, and long ago, of Miss Hattie's poem in *The Glove Trade Gazette*? In the sense that Charles Lamb extended the bounds of literature to encompass "draught-boards, bound and lettered on the back," is it not possible that the rewards of a Dear Abbie and a Dostoievsky vary not in kind but only in degree?

Despite the good Doctor Johnson, who loved to simplify issues, I do not believe that in any but the most rare and accidental cases did the desire for money precede the desire to write. Not today, and not in Johnson's day, would any sane person with an empty stomach turn to writing as a sure and speedy means of filling it.

Goldsmith, at his wits' end to find money for his rent, was mad to sit scribbling at *The Vicar of Wakefield* instead of seeking employment as a clerk. His neighbours (and assuredly his landlady) would have condemned him as lazy and shiftless. I know of Canadian writers of whom the same thing has been said because they were dedicated enough (or crazy enough, depending on the viewpoint) to refuse to squander their time and talent over ledgers or assembly lines. The chance of Goldsmith's good fairy so opportunely arriving, even in the improbable guise of Sam Johnson, to convert the manuscript into sixty pounds hard cash, was so remote that it could not be said that Goldsmith was making any serious attempt to meet his obligations. It would have been less reprehensible, and the odds would have been more in his favour, had he taken to the highway.

There have doubtless been those to whom the desire for money and the urge to write presented themselves as coexistent itches that might be scratched at the same time. Some of these would succeed at making money and a few — since according to Sartre we live on an edge of choice — would come in time to think less of money and more of writing until the fine madness possessed them quite. And many the others who, beginning with the literary virus in their blood, have found their writing prematurely profitable, and money has proved for them an effective antitoxin that has enabled them to retain their health, sanity, and social respectability, following a comfortable and profitable rut into their ripe and unregretting age. In general, however, the lure of riches is the destroyer rather than the developer of genius.

Fame, then? Doubtless there is an ingredient of this. To want to be a writer is to want to be a pre-eminent one, just as to wish to be an architect is to dream of being a greater Wren. But, like the desire for money, it is a conditional desire, and no true artist would wilfully sacrifice integrity to attain it. Another great fallacy is that a person becomes a writer because of some Messial message that chafes within, and must out. Many indeed have been beguiled into literature because, while unburdening themselves of such a message, they have, like hospital patients, become conditioned to their medicine. They have discovered the addictive pleasures of the pen. But commonly the urge to write exists long before the idea of what to write about. It is usual to think of writing as merely a vehicle to convey the idea, but in truth the idea is a convenient medium for the fulfilment of the desire to write.

The need for "self-expression" also is often blamed for all the writers in the world, and this is so vague a concept that it is difficult to refute. In the sense of "self-fulfillment" it is to some extent true. "One's wish for the work of art," wrote Brigid Brophy, "is not that it should be understood, but that it should be loved — loved not by others merely, or even preferably, but by oneself; one writes the novel to please one's own self-love. Just as it is more lasting, so it is more beautiful than one's original self. It is a receptacle for one's own narcissism, which is often so ill-served by one's proper Ego."

Like all the other pseudo-explanations, this reveals but one aspect of the truth. The hint of a desire for permanence is significant. The urge to write is almost a religious one, begotten of a need to believe in something more permanent than one's own transient being, in something that will not be shed and forgotten in the autumn of the flesh. It is a bid to triumph over death; not only the death of self but the death of things and of moments — a desperate ache to preserve, a revolt against change and decay. It is an ache for the permanence not of things themselves but of one's own experience of things: a desire, perhaps, to perpetuate one's own consciousness. Is this not, after all, the basis of all religion?

But this again is but one tatter from the mantle of truth, and we end up very much where we began, with the conviction that writers write because they want to, because they must.

Books on the Shelf?

It is maintained in some quarters that literature is doomed except as an adjunct to more modern arts of communication. Books are to be put, so to speak, on the shelf. There are people who see the writer of tomorrow as no more than a producer of scripts to be turned into electronic pablum for mass audiences, for whom the book will appear no more practical as a means of getting ideas across from one person to another than is the horse and buggy as a means of getting to the moon.

And indeed, there are writers who have found the economic pressures so great and the meed of appreciation so small, that they have abandoned the ship without even bothering to pump. No doubt from the profitable anonymity of the credit lists that flit unheeded by as we leave the cinema or chase the children to bed, these writers dream of a comeback to the arena of literary glory — after they have made their pile. Invariably they seem surprised to discover — if they ever do — that what they have bartered for their years of success has been the very self out of which their masterpieces might have grown.

The book, it has been suggested, is old-fashioned and inefficient. One's reactionary tendency to question the need for efficiency in enjoyment is quickly overborne by the fanfare that heralds the dawn of the era of more direct and comprehensive communication. Comment though we may, a little wryly, that it has been dawning for a long time without shedding any light into our snug, bookish gloom, we nevertheless find ourselves half-persuaded that modern gadgetry and gimmickry can penetrate to depths of sensibility — and to profundities of ignorance — that have hitherto defied the assault of the most formidable literary genius.

Yet, the McLuhans and mixed-media fanatics of this world notwithstanding, the literary constitution rejects these alien organisms we seek to graft upon it; and for a simple, self-evident reason. Old fashioned the book may be: inefficient it is not. Its greatest virtue, by comparison with any of the hybrid media in which we may seek to combine it, is the directness of communication between the mind that conceives the idea and the mind that ultimately receives it. It needs no promoters, no high-priced middle men, no interpreters, no stars or supernumaries, no props, no bite of the gross national product. It might indeed be demonstrated that the clarity and force with which any artistic proposition is transmitted between two minds is in inverse proportion to the persons and paraphernalia interposed between them. For if the receiving mind is alert and well disposed, such extraneous influences can only be a hindrance: if it is stodgy and reluctant it will gladly submit to being passively amused, but no amount of spoon feeding will nourish it. Understanding and appreciation demand effort, and this effort is discouraged by the passive media.

Both the book as an object and literature as a medium have peculiar and inalienable qualities which guarantee their survival and independence in face of all competition, all change. Literature is the most enduring of the arts. It is virtually indestructible by anything but its own insufficiency. It is accessible without fuss or significant expense, and the experience it offers is repeatable at will, in whole or in part, at any time, at any pace: its bounty is never exhausted. For the writer it offers a sense of creation, of fulfillment that is not attainable through writing for the cinema or television. Arthur Hailey is an excellent television writer and but a mediocre novelist, but it was the hunger for permanence and this kind of fulfillment that lured him from his natural though not wholly satisfying medium. He told me of the morning he asked a friend's opinion of his play broadcast the previous night. "What play?" he was asked. He was powerless to reproduce the experience for his friend. Well he might ask himself whether it were not perhaps better to have written a second-rate book that he could at least put into his friend's hand. Perhaps his choice was wrong, but it was very natural.

One advantage the written word has over all the artificial means by which we seek to transmit it is that it can cater to any minority, however small. The great peril of television is that it is economically constrained within limits related to the lowest common denominator of taste. Literature requires but an audience of one to be viable and justified. Many great works have been rescued from oblivion by the dedication of one enthusiast.

It is for an audience of one, after all, that a book is created. It never reaches more. No two persons can read the same book, any more than they can occupy the same situation in space and time. What the book is to them is conditioned by all their earlier experience, by the associations they involuntarily attach to language, by the place and time at which they read it, by the state of their health, by what they had for dinner. Reading thus offers an intensely personal experience — thank God! — in the midst of what we aptly and ominously call "mass media." For this reason, if for no other, literature will and must pursue an independent existence.

The Screening Process

The advent of the film has no doubt affected the course of literature in many subtle ways, and in some ways not so subtle. New techniques that were dictated or inspired by this sudden emancipation of the drama from the rigid limits of the stage gave new dimensions to the use of language and opened up splendid vistas of narrative technique. Such influences as these, since they enrich the creative process, could only be good, and strangely enough they produced the most salutary effects in writing that was neither intended for nor adaptable to the screen.

Other effects were less admirable. Writers whose legacy of books might have won them lasting repute sacrificed their destiny for an easy dollar and a fleeting credit line. Others still wrote their film scripts in the form of novels, but they were very much aware of Sam Goldwyn peering over their shoulders as they wrote. These were the shrewd ones who wanted to eat their cake and have it. They laid up for themselves treasures on earth, but not without a wistful eye on the heaven of literary immortality.

But the effect of films on books was not confined to the work of contemporary authors. Before Hollywood, the growth and decline of literary reputation was an orderly if not a predictable process. Whatever the initial impact of a book, it was almost invariably doomed to a period of obscurity, of eclipse; of purgatory, if you will. From this oblivion many never more emerged. They died, so to speak, in their sleep. Others were rescued from beneath the settling dust of human apathy and forgetfulness by the persisting enthusiasm and sleepless curiosity of those whom Arnold Bennett called "the passionate few."

This orderly refinement through the expanding mesh of time underwent a violent upset as the screen's appetite for new stories grew. Some books that would have been deservedly forgotten in a year, like *Peyton Place*, will now persist in this generation's blood and consciousness like the memory of measles. Others were exhumed from forgotten graves. Still others, which enjoyed a secure place in literary history but were never more than names to the average person — *Tom Jones*, to take but one example — suddenly were thrust upon the popular notice and sprouted belated best-selling editions.

A latecomer to this last group was Conrad's *Lord Jim*. It was in a way an improbable choice for a film (as was Joyce's *Ulysses*), and it would have taken a genius as great as Conrad's own to translate the spirit and the significance of the story into the new medium; for the power of the book stems less from the eventfulness of its plot than from the author's unique style and from the superb obliqueness of the narrative method.

This obliqueness, so vital to this and many of Conrad's other works, tends to alienate some readers. The first piece of writing I ever sold was an essay on Conrad, whose work had a profound effect on me at a time when it was entering its period of eclipse. And the editor, in accepting it, said that he had not previously cared much for Conrad because he needlessly complicated his narration by having A tell B the story of C, often learned at second hand from D, E and F. Such failure to appreciate the purpose of this device and the superlative skill with which it was used astounded me; for it was the recognition of this artistry, together with Conrad's new and potent use of the English language, that had held me spellbound while my mother cried in vain that it was time for supper.

There has been a striking resemblance between the popular response to the film and the early reaction to Conrad as a writer, perhaps because both readers and audience had been encouraged to expect the wrong things. The film was advertised as being adventurous and exotic, just as thirty years before it was customary to acclaim Conrad as a great writer of epics of the sea. All these things are of course true, but they are significantly true only because they are incidental. The reader or viewer who makes them his only criteria is likely to be disappointed.

Conrad himself recognized this defect in the popular awareness, particularly with regard to the significance of the sea in his work. To his friend Richard Curle, who was writing an article about him, he wrote, "Do try and keep the damned sea out if you can. My interests are terrestrial, after all." And this was true. He loved the sea and he loved ships — inevitably, for they had made him — but they were the environment and material of his work, not the reason for its existence. He would probably have written books equally great had destiny thrown him among soldiers, miners or clerks.

It was to our good fortune, and to the good fortune of literature, that fate led him to the sea, for there life was lived at its simplest, and the conflict of moral strength with adverse destiny could be discerned through a minimum of obscuring influences. A ship at sea was a world in miniature, harbouring all the greater world's passion and fatalism but few of its petty distractions. But Conrad had no romantic delusions about "the sea that gives nothing but hard knocks, and sometimes a chance to show your strength."

For several years critics followed each other like sheep in acclaiming Conrad's genius but asserting that his work was "outside the main stream of English literature." But this was obviously nonsense. His influence upon those who followed has been profound, even though unacknowledged, and has manifested itself in some unexpected places; not least in the work of Graham Greene. In this age of preoccupation with "facts"; in this age of passive submission to the allure of the screen, Conrad, along with the passionate few, may well prove to be one of the forces that keep the art of fiction alive.

5

The Mother Tongue

The Ize Age

The Ize Age is upon us. Thanks to the wizards of biz, at whose well-heeled feet even language may be made to cringe, we now have a magic formula by which we can transform any part of speech into a verb, without knowledge of grammar, without effort of thought, without fear of error.

One has but to cast a glance at the hoardings along the street to learn the simple rule: the five-foot steak sizzling there above the sidewalk has been tenderized; the skin cream in the hand of the towering beauty who takes her bath at the street corner has been moisturized; the tissues responsible for the contented expression at both ends of the immense baby over the bank are softerized. It is all so easy that in no time at all we shall be able to dispense with English classes in schools and concentrate on learning French. We shall have to. Our own language will have become so ugly and stunted that only advertising people and scientists will want to use it.

It will no doubt pleasurize the dead-language scholar of the future to realize that English is regularized to possibilize the verbizing of the whole language by one simplerized and standardized rule that will minimize the effort to memorize; to find the language, in a word, instantized. I cannot take credit for this last, this ultimate gem of philology, this word that surely above all others speaks for and sums up our age.

No, I stole it from a flour bag. I would have said I plagiarized it, but the word turned my stomach. But what may make that scholar less happy will be the discovery that a language so convenient and easy to learn is for any evocative purpose dead; dead of a stealthy poison that transmutes its rich, life-giving diversity into a fatal monotony.

But whence comes this great need we feel to transform innocent adjectives and nouns into verbs? Is it perhaps that we are becoming, increasingly, people of action rather than contemplation? Strange, if we are, for contemplation is the one thing our machines cannot do for us. Or is it that in this bustling age of efficiency we are working towards the principle that every idea must be reducible to a single word?

How else, for example, can we explain the compulsion that is upon us to say we are hospitalized, instead of in hospital? It requires fewer letters and less respiratory effort to say "in hospital", and certainly the sound is less harsh.

Could this be a symptom of our growing worship of the automatic? Is it part of our desire to reduce everything to a comfortable system that demands neither thought nor effort; all people to pawns that can be pushed around and rearranged to conform to the pattern of the game without unreasonable and inconvenient resistance from their individuality? "Hospitalize" is something we can do to Mr. Smith, whereas only he can be in hospital. By being in hospital he is asserting himself as a separate and sovereign being: an inconvenient thing when he is there at our expense. If we as taxpayers are going to share the bill, we have a right to hospitalize him, as we might broil a steak (tenderized). Our science-oriented minds are increasingly impatient of anything that resists classification.

I would suggest that the trend stems in part from our old enemy, the unwarranted generalization. Our mentors so labour the point that the active is preferable to the passive that language has become aggressive. It masters us instead of being our servant. It becomes a bludgeon to strike the reason senseless, rather than a torch to light the way to understanding.

Again, perhaps it is an unconscious attempt to make amends to the language for what we and our American friends have done to it. We have done our best to destroy what little order existed in English by simplifying spelling, by being too anxious that it should appear logical and consistent, thus divorcing words not only from the ancestry by which they might be identified, but from the extant members of their own family. People began to write "harbor" to disguise from themselves the deplorable fact that they were too lazy to pronounce "harbour." What in fact they do say is "harber", so why not be completely honest and logical and spell it that way?

Now, belatedly, we seem to be seeking to restore order to the language by tagging to every word a common suffix that will give the most ignorant and inarticulate command of the English language. Unfortunately the omnipotent "ize" demands emphasis, and overpowers every word to which it is attached. It is a parasitic growth upon the language that will sap its vitality and render its development grotesque.

I do not suppose that we as individual men and women of this generation are any more lax in the use of language than our forebears were. There is always, in any language, a lively vernacular ferment out of which the dross settles slowly to leave the formal tongue clear and potent. In the past, writers and orators have used only the bright, pure liquor, and so maintained the glory and stability of their tongue. But now the language becomes more and more the tool of technology and the slave of commerce. Others usurp the stewardship of language that once belonged to the makers of literature, and stir up continually the sediment of jargon and slang.

But why all this concern? It is true that a writer, witnessing this violence to his language, feels as a painter might who stood helpless while vandals befouled the colours on his palette, or a musician while his instrument was being tuned by a tone-deaf monkey. Worse, for a word's virtue is no more recoverable than a woman's. Never again, when the spirit of gaiety moves us, shall we dare admit to being gay. A writer cannot but be aware that unless this tendency to corruption is resisted, our language will be doomed as a literary instrument. It will lose its subtlety, its flexibility, its power. It will no longer be capable of ensnaring in its precise poetic net the elusive ideas that wing from heart to heart through the sluggish minds of men.

But what of the general public, for whom language is like — but far less important than — money; a mere currency by means of which one may purchase a pound of information or an ounce of understanding? What is all this worry about words to them? Whether they are aware of it or not, it is very much their concern, for no people can be great that has a corrupt or enfeebled language. The whole character and outlook of a nation is affected by its language. How can a tongue that is shaped by the jargon of the supermarket fail in its turn to shape those that use it as their means of everyday communication?

From time to time a champion emerges and rides to the rescue of the fair language in distress, but usually the attempt is met with a shocking apathy. No one seems to care. In an age when truth is much talked about, few pause to consider that precision of language is the key to truth, and that corruption of language can be as disastrous to a people as the corruption of morals.

In Defence of Adjectives

The adjective is surely the most maligned of all the parts of speech. All the stylistic sins of the inept are laid at its door. There is a belief abroad even among otherwise intelligent teachers of language and literature that any piece of writing will be improved and rendered more forceful and effective by the ruthless deletion of its adjectives. Some very convincing examples can be adduced in support of this contention, and unless one is of suspicious temper where such cure-all formulae are concerned, it is easy to be blinded to the fact that it is not the adjective but its wrongful use that offends.

Since my earliest inklings of the power and beauty of words, which came long before I knew how to harness the one or aspire to the other, I have been of the conviction that the adjective is as noble and necessary a part of language as any other. From seeing it thus persistently and often ignorantly reviled I have developed a sympathy for it, and am perhaps more partial in its defence than I might otherwise be. Injustice ever begets indignation. Despite all the efforts of sedulous pedantry to obscure the fact, I soon discovered that the humble adjective could be as potent in its place as the most earthy of verbs or the most Anglo-Saxon of nouns.

I am aware that one of my favourite passages in all literature, that begins: "Consider the lilies of the field, how they grow: they toil not, neither do they spin..." contains not a single direct adjective, and I would be the first to admit that there is no adjective in the language that could be inserted anywhere in the passage without destroying it; but I am also aware that had the intent of the writer been different, if he had wanted to capture the beauty of the lilies for his reader instead of wishing merely to avail himself of their familiar image for purposes of comparison, not all the verbs and nouns in his vocabulary could have evoked their fragile loveliness. Because the adjective misused can emasculate style, there are those that believe it must always be resisted, admitted into composition but in the direst extremities, and then only in the status of a necessary evil. This sort of foolishness results from the desire of the clinically inclined to reduce everything to order. How simple and straightforward life would be for writer, reader and critic if literature could be reduced to rule of thumb. These pseudo-logicians see the world as a great laboratory. They make a few random observations of this or that, plot their mental graph and extend it to infinity. No one questions the validity of their monstrous assumptions.

Detractors of the adjective thunder the great passages of literature to labour the point that simplicity is power. It is a point of some validity, but like most unwarranted generalizations it is made by presenting only the facts that fit the case, and ignoring those that threaten it. Mark Anthony's funeral oration has power. Its nouns and verbs roll Churchillian from the tongue to hold listeners in thrall:

Friends, Romans, countrymen, lend me your ears;
I come to bury Caesar, not to praise him...

But this is only one sort of power, the power of oratory, of exhortation. It is a power achieved through event, through action. Obviously this is the province of the verb and noun. Even here, however, the adjective, judiciously used, can hold its own:

Break, break, break,
On thy cold gray stones, O sea!

Would anyone be foolish enough to suggest that this line is weakened by its double adjective? But even if action can dispense with the adjective, there is more to life, more to literature — more, certainly, to poetry — than mere event.

There is many and many a passage that, achieving grandeur by the austere march of its nouns and verbs, would deflate like a balloon if its one leavening adjective were taken away:

> To be or not to be,
> That is the question.
> Whether 'tis nobler in the mind to suffer
> The slings and arrows of ignoble fortune...

Simplicity is often a source of strength and dignity, but the sort of simplicity that eschews adjectives can also be oppressively austere. Its effect is rather like that of mountain peaks. They are beautiful and majestic, but they are only so in relation to the fruitful valleys and plains. Without such relief they become in vast expanses tiring and a little terrifying. But it is in any case a great fallacy — though commonly believed — that simplicity is precluded by the use of adjectives. Certainly power is not.

The adjective is to literature what colour is to painting. Nobility of form can be depicted in black and white, often to advantage, but in many cases the work does not come fully and excitingly to life until the artist uses colour. Often an adjective fills out the rhythm and transforms a true but colourless statement into noble and memorable poetry or prose, as witness Homer's

> Thundering he fell,
> And loud his armour rang.

The power of the adjective is the power of evocation. Without adjectives no description is possible except through simile and metaphor, and without description, precise visual images can not be evoked. It is commonly suggested that description impedes the narrative flow, but this is true only when the description is ponderous and inept. The best description is however seldom direct, and is usually most effective when it is oblique, circumspect. And this quality is vital to any composition that involves the use of adjectives. He may be safe from error who avoids the adjective, but he only can be called a master who uses it with subtlety and skill.

If anyone still doubts the potency of adjectives, and believes that the writer is better off without them, I suggest that he might take one of the more important prose works of Dylan Thomas, delete all the adjectives that can be removed without destroying the continuity of the narrative, and then read aloud what, if anything, is left.

Philosophy and Style

Technique is the father of philosophy. One cannot persist long on the use of words as materials of art without becoming to some degree aware of this. It is a disturbing awareness, which many writers have attempted in various ways to communicate, or have unwittingly acknowledged in passing. But reduced thus to its essence it becomes a preposterous statement, a rash paradox upon which a budding doctor of literature might build a thesis and a substantial reputation without danger of being taken seriously, and without perhaps suspecting the profound truth underlying it.

There comes time when what one says, however significant it may be, is recognized as being less important than one's manner of saying it. Usually one glimpses this early. Indeed, it is the source of the strange, irrational compulsion to write. But then it is lost sight of, like Wordsworth's clouds of glory, sometimes never to be glimpsed again. Lured by it into the addiction of the pen, many a man (and, lately, many, many a woman) scribbles away uninspired years of platitudes, communicating information but no knowledge,

> As if his whole vocation
> Were endless imitation.

A few artists grope their way back to it, blindly, by instinct and with much labour. They acquire the assurance of it at last as a violinist attains to his vibrato, not knowing whence it came but finding it, once come, involuntary and very sweet upon the ear. Yesterday they wrote: today they have style. Tomorrow a philosophy. Henceforth style rules, and all their thought and endeavour, their very perception, is shaped by it. Their awareness is sharpened to a new focus. The Dublin of *Ulysses* was not the Dublin of Leopold Bloom but the Dublin of James Joyce possessed of stylistic spectacles, changed but made more surely itself by the manner of capturing it.

This growth of philosophy out of style has been typified in the career of Alain Robbe-Grillet, the French novelist defensively turned critic. As he wrote, gaining the feel of his pen, he found himself adopting with increasing assurance a sparse, dispassionate style that allowed no compromise with reality. To the casual reader this writing is simple, unadorned, stark, often repetitive, and diamond hard. It is wilfully devoid of metaphor, and it commits the extravagance of an adjective only as a chemist might, to convey a physical property that has been incontrovertibly established.

This manner of writing sometimes defeats its own potential monotony and gains considerable power. It exerts a strange fascination. One becomes slowly aware that it is more than just a way of using words. It is a way of seeing life. It imposes its own necessities upon the author and upon the world around him. Deprived of all the subjective devices that elicit the readiest responses but tend to cloud the vision, M. Robbe-Grillet is reduced to describing the surfaces of things. Objects are allowed only to exist. They are permitted to enter the minds of persons only as naked perceptions. The eye sees but the mind does not make judgments. Nor does it seek to project significance into objects which, considered simply as objects, they cannot be said to possess. They are not compared with other objects for fear of suggesting a connection that does not exist. One thing is not as big or as small as another. It is defined by its unique shape and dimension, and no assumptions are made concerning its interior or even its unseen sides. Nothing is altered by the observer's attitude to it or conception of it.

The starkness of this technique inevitably aroused criticism and even hostility. M. Robbe-Grillet — all innocence and concern to be understood — came to its defence in a brief essay or two in literary periodicals. These were misunderstood and attacked in their turn. The author elaborated and there slowly emerged, in the course of this interplay of criticism, self-examination and justification, M. Robbe-Grillet's working philosophy. It would be easy to assume that this philosophy existed before the author put pen to paper, and that his style evolved to meet its stringencies. Indeed, the essays tend to suggest this, but it is very evidently not true. Most of the criticism arose from the camp of the humanists. Any style which declines to allow the mind to invade the uniqueness, the self-sufficiency of inanimate objects is bound to appear as a belittlement of man, as a challenge to his position as the being with relation to whom all else exists. Robbe-Grillet thus emerges as an anti-humanist, and in becoming perforce defensive he has become dogmatic.

He has been backed into a position of declaring in effect that his gospel of verbal chastity is inviolable and that all metaphor is sin. Any literary device that tends to bestow significance upon physical objects, to ascribe to them any importance other than that of simply being there to be seen or bumped into, is held as being something to be avoided, not only by M. Robbe-Grillet but by all who take the art of fiction seriously.

Ironically enough, M. Robbe-Grillet is defeated by his own zeal. The very nakedness of his reference to external objects, and in particular his repetitions, confer in increasing measure the significance he seeks to avoid. Perhaps it is merely that we as readers are conditioned to seek such significance. At any rate we cannot avoid finding it there.

Quotation: Its Use and Abuse

One has but to glance at current trends in criticism to conclude that quotations, like statistics, can be made to prove anything. There are two cults in particular, equally ingenious and equally futile, which use this device to establish improbable connections that do little for literature and even less for the edification of the reader.

The first of these might be called criticism by comparison. It consists in taking two or more writers and seeking to prove by liberal quotation that they are stylistically, or philosophically, or psychologically or in some less obvious way alike. Or that they are not. It is good sport, and with practice one can acquire considerable finesse, not unlike a juggler's. To manipulate two authors is clever but comparatively simple. Three is more difficult. To keep four in the air at the same time bespeaks erudition and lifelong study.

The other method is what I call criticism by analogy. It calls for more synthetic imagination than the other, a greater power of putting together an improbable two and two. In this approach, one needs not only two or more writers, or sometimes two or more individual works, but some sort of unifying theme by which their creative blood-relationship may be demonstrated. Thus it is possible, though of dubious critical value, to show that three extremely secular works are subconscious variations on the passion of Christ, or that two writers who thought they were producing novels about the innocent and utterly dissimilar years of their childhood were in fact merely plagiarizing *Oedipus Rex*. I recall reading many years ago in a prestigious American magazine a letter from a well-known novelist, denying the allegation of a critic (also well-known) that the underlying theme of his book was homosexuality. Nothing, said the author, had been further from his mind. But the critic with colossal arrogance responded that although the author may not have known he was writing about homosexuality, he had in fact done exactly that.

I suspect that the reason for this spate of pseudo-criticism is the compulsion so many scholars find themselves under to produce theses in literature. It is difficult indeed to say something substantial and new about the work of a single writer whose renown may not be called in question: but to establish a relationship between two of them demands only diligence. No one is likely to question the comparison so long as it has at least a superficial validity. This is harmless enough. True, it tends to spoil our appetite for the writers in question, and it introduces a refraction into our view which ensures that we shall never see them true again, never be able to shake them free of the double image that has been gratuitously suggested. But then, who reads theses? Unfortunately we all do, increasingly. These comparisons become so fascinating to their "discoverers" that they cannot leave them alone. They become a sort of literary itch that must be scratched continually. With one eye on a professorship and the other on a literary reputation, these self-styled critics perceive their analogies suddenly as geese that will lay their golden eggs *ad infinitum*. And, unhappily, *ad nauseum*. What was laboriously conceived as an expedient on the hard road to a Ph.D takes on the glow of a divine revelation. The thesis becomes an article in a literary magazine. A letter to the editor provokes a second, and in no time at all the writer of this questionable stuff becomes a specialist in the relationship between two writers who wanted above all simply to be themselves. The elaboration of this theme becomes the writer's life-work. And it is all done by the simple manipulation of quotations.

But this is only one example of the abuse of the art of quotation. It is, indeed, an art. It is an art that has few successful exponents but many, many abusers. One quotes to impart to one's own work the flavour of another's thought; but to be used with profit and without taint of plagiarism the quoted passage should come as spontaneously as one's own thought, should have been so assimilated into one's consciousness that it comes forth embedded in the new work like a fossil, so intimately impressed and so long accepted that while retaining its identity it is inseparable from the native rock of the present writer's own conviction. In its truest and highest form quotation should enhance both the new words and the old. It should impart a new depth of lustre and a new significance.

How often a wise or well-turned thought lies buried self-effacing in its context until it appears illuminated and as it were fulfilled in the work of another, as a woman's beauty kindles to a sincere compliment. Quotation of this spontaneous sort is perhaps the truest and highest criticism; the recognition and applause of excellence by a kindred spirit. For as Anatole France remarked, "The good critic is he who relates the adventures of his soul among masterpieces." What worthier applause could one offer the work of another than to make it truly part of one's own?

But the abuses of quotation are many. After all, it is profitable at ten cents a word. It can be used with negligible mental effort to pad one's own work out to the required length while lending the weight of another's authority to one's own dubious conclusions. It can be used to prove a point — valid or otherwise — or to bolster a shaky analogy. It can be taken as the text of a literary sermon. It may even be used to advertise a deodorant.

One of the less admirable uses of quotation is to be found in those articles that recur infallibly with the seasons, replete with quotation but devoid alike of spirit and substance. They take the time of year, or a seasonal activity, or the migration of birds, and use it as an excuse for a miniature anthology of quotations strung together on a skein of uninspired narrative. The labour and mechanics of composition are so distressingly evident that instead of being carried away by the quotations' leap into lyricism, the delicate fabric of literary illusion is destroyed by an image of the author, six inches from page's end and minutes from his deadline, reaching desperately for his Bartlett.

These hodgepodge pieces attain a certain vapid unity, a certain passing appeal. We accept them as inevitable, like dandelions. We have come to expect a bunch of spring quotations, neatly arranged in the likeness of an essay, as we expect a nosegay of wild flowers from our children: with only the difference that this year's flowers lose nothing by being exactly the same as last year's, while trite essays lose a great deal.

State of the Art

The word "art" is probably the most misused in the language. Because of its broad connotation, its extreme subjectivity and its defiance of comprehensive definition, it lends itself to abuse by the slipshod writer and the woolly thinker. It has a convenient suggestion of mystery that dignifies anything to which it is applied, while relieving the user of the obligation to be precise. It tempts us to enjoy the licence of the artist without accepting his responsibilities. The word is surrounded by jungles of subjective association in which, after speaking airily of the art of camping, or the art of stick handling, or even, (incredible but true) the art of statistical analysis, one may take refuge with impunity.

Because of this susceptibility to abuse there is a temptation to define the word for present use; but so many good intentions have died in the attempt, and I am in any case so suspicious of those learned gentlemen who cannot use one word without mustering a whole army of others to make it do its duty, that I do not wish to become one of their number. I sympathize with these gentlemen, lawyers for the most part, who cannot trust words because they cannot trust each other, and the growing army of semanticists who swarm and botanize upon the fruitful fields of literature.

I appreciate their problem, which is to be precise. But communication is an act of faith. At its highest, it is an inspired act of faith: faith in the bond of humanity and the mysterious chemistry of perception that enables us, like plants, to draw our common sustenance of truth and understanding from the diverse soils in which we grow.

Language is effective only to the extent that we trust one another to receive it, and it loses its potency when this trust is not present. Confined in the toils of finicking qualification, it dies. The moment a person starts to define words before using them, we may be sure that he is about to stifle the sympathetic forces of imagination that alone make understanding possible. Communication is a high-wire act: if we do not have the faith, and if the person on the other trapeze has not been conditioned to the point of instinct to receive us, not all the mathematical tracing of trajectories nor all the calculation of forces in the world will bring us together.

But to return to art. It all began with an impulse to talk about "the art of reading", and an immediate reaction of inquiry into what the term implied. For my chief complaint against the abusers of the word is that they use it to denote the skill or the esoterics of a field of activity; what the jargoneers in their reluctance to call a spade a spade like to refer to as "expertise." Having dignified their subject with the title of an art, they immediately disqualify it, and demonstrate that they have no inkling what the word implies by seeking to lay down rules or to give precise instructions for the practise of the so-called art. This, of course, one cannot do: for the essence of art is that it knows no rule but that of absolute and intuitive self-reliance, that it takes no instruction but from that all-wise and infallible mentor, the imagination.

There may well be an art of camping, though I doubt if there are many practitioners of it. I do not close the door entirely upon an art of stick-handling, though I cannot conceive it. But an art of statistical analysis would turn the whole world of the good Dr. Gallup upside-down, and raise such a dust in our automated world that all the computers would be clogged to a standstill.

And so at last to the art of reading. I am no Quiller-Couch, equipped to discourse at length upon the subject without plunging into the pitfalls I have been at such pains to point out. Reading is indeed capable of being refined into an art, but there are no rules for attaining the pleasures of it.

It is an art in the sense that its practice is something to be perfected on one's own terms, to be evolved out of one's own personality. As with any art, it is a highly personal thing that cannot be taught, cannot even be demonstrated. One can only give vague intimations, give free rein to one's enthusiasm and live, fervently and with quiet assurance, the literate life in the hope that conviction will beget emulation.

Certainly the art of reading is not to be mastered through the massive "reading programs" that well-meaning university professors, at the instigation of dollar-hungry publishers, offer us through lavish advertisements in literary magazines. These regiments of books that parade so nobly and so expensively colourful across the double-page spread fire us with ambition to be well read, fill us with wanderlust for the unexplored continents of literature. But what a dead weight they are upon our shelves and upon our conscience when the monthly payment, falling inexorably due, reminds us that we have turned more pages in our cheque-book than in the *Treasury of the World's Great Books*.

Reading programs are admirable in theory, and might well be of value had we the will and the fortitude to carry them out; but their very ponderousness and rigidity kills the appetite they are intended to excite. They fail because they seek to impose upon the art of reading the discipline of a science. Reading, like making friends, is a random, unpredictable process, and a program of reading is no more likely to yield the desired result than a program for meeting soul-mates. In reading, as in making friends, we are likely to find the highest rewards where we find the highest enjoyment, and to be most successful when we are being most truly ourselves.

Simplicity and Precision

Much of our modern writing seems to be characterized more by sensational content than by vigour of style. However strenuously it may be argued that content and style are inseparable, one comes increasingly to suspect that there are writers of considerable repute who rely upon the sensational appeal of their material to disguise from themselves and from others that they have never mastered their language. They have no style of their own, and if they are distinguished at all it is in their extreme timidity in the use of words.

There are two extremities of evil to which literature is prone: feebleness of thought obscured by complexity of language, and complexity of thought obscured by feebleness of language. But some of our contemporaries are too cautious to be guilty of either: they match their feebleness of thought by their feebleness of language, and obscure both by clubbing the reader's sensibilities to death with sensation. They assure others, and would like to convince themselves, that all this talk of style is mere affectation. They are great sticklers for simplicity. In all probability they subscribed to the follies of the *Fog Index*, now mercifully, it appears, laid to rest.

Simplicity is an admirable quality, in literature as in all things. It has been too often and with too much wisdom extolled for me to gainsay it, even should I so wish, but like other assertions by the wise, it is prone to abuse by the foolish. In writing, as in dress, there is the simplicity of taste and the simplicity of slovenliness. Too often, the plea of simplicity is merely an excuse for evading the trouble of saying what we truly mean: or rather, of deciding what we mean; for we do not know what we mean until we have precisely framed our thought.

It is paradoxical that we should need to define simplicity, but it is evident that many of its advocates have never paused to consider what it is. Too many people when they speak of simplicity really mean "easiness", when in fact the simpler a work of art is, the greater the demands it makes upon both the one that produces it and those who would appreciate it. It is a great mistake to assume that simplicity absolves us from effort in composition or in comprehension. One of the wisest observations ever made on the subject of style was that of Robert Louis Stevenson: "Out of fulness of thinking, expression drops perfect like a ripe fruit."

Surely by simplicity we mean, ultimately, the best way of framing what we have in mind, the paring away of inessentials. We do not mean austerity, or childishness of vocabulary, or superficiality. We should never abandon the pursuit of meaning or the struggle for precise expression because simple language will not suffice for it. The simplest way of coming at an idea, of conveying a nuance of meaning, may be through complexity. The complexity may well be a necessary part of the experience, as in the work of Henry James. Our delight in the convolution of his language is essential to our enjoyment. It is the only means by which he might have produced that particular effect, and conveyed to the mind of his reader what was so clear in his own.

The highest form of "simplicity" is that which is simple at all levels of comprehension, as in the work of Malcolm Lowry, or of any poet whose work is memorable. At the lower levels we merely miss the allusions, remain deaf to the echoes, are innocent of the subtleties, but we enjoy and are uplifted still. In this respect, James Joyce's *Ulysses* is something of a failure, for while it delights those who share the author's erudition and are aware of the diversities of his experience, it offers little to the receptive but unsophisticated mind.

Most people who extol and demand simplicity do not give a fig for it. What they want is avoidance of the unusual. They do not want us to overtax their attention, to make demands upon their thought. They want to reach the summit, but they resent the effort of the climb. The pastures are sweeter up there, but they are too lazy to stray beyond the well-cropped plains of cliché and colloquial phrase. The well-cropped pasture, however, provides lean fare.

Many writers have spoken with contempt — even as they polished — of "polishing periods." But it is in this process of polishing, of finding the ultimately appropriate word or phrase, that the elusive hare of meaning is started, and run at last to earth. What folly and presumption to imagine that we can build a cathedral by taking bricks of any shape and size that happen to be lying around, and placing them one upon another without thought.

It is strange that this doctrine of false simplicity should have such currency. There are, after all, so many works of genius that argue against it. "Ah, yes," we are taught. "So-and-so broke the rules, but he was a genius." There is a smug assumption that genius could not possibly be present in our classrooms; or that genius, like sainthood, is only posthumously conferred; or that it comes into the world certified with an academic brand upon its buttocks. At what point in his career, I used to wonder, did old Shakespeare acquire the infernal gall to imagine himself a genius, to be breaking all the rules that the rest of us must follow?

But one lesson among many we may learn from the fate of Shakespeare is that, if we take great pains to say something in the best possible way, if we labour, that is to say, to make it simple, we may be sure that generations of scholars will devote themselves to proving it is not.

Experience and Expression

Between Lawrence Durrell's assertion that a novelist should know many countries and Thoreau's "I have travelled widely — in Concord" there is a world of speculation. How much experience does a writer need? We discussed this question at length one day, to the neglect of our lunch, and all the time I was aware of something echoing. It was the title of that savagely ironical story by Tolstoy: "How Much Land Does a Man Need?" And although our discussion ranged wide and plumbed deep, starting many philosophical foxes without bringing any to earth, I became increasingly convinced that the answer to Tolstoy's question and our own was the same: very little.

It all arose from my companion's complaint that it is difficult to find time to read sufficient to keep abreast of what is going on in the world of letters, and my innocent doubting of any real need for such awareness. Like many barbs that deflate presumptions, my question was rhetorical, even jocular. But flippant questions have a way of rankling, of proliferating. What is this great compulsion that is upon us to know what others are doing before we do anything ourselves? Does one necessarily write any better for being aware what (as opposed to how) others are writing? Or having a clear and synthetic awareness of current trends? Would our writers be better and more productive if they flocked in groups of a literary feather, or formed schools, as painters tend to do?

There are of course many reasons why a writer must read, but the least important of these, it seems to me, is the need to keep up with "what is going on." He must read, especially when he is young, to feed his love of language. He learns to write by ear, by the concordance of beautiful words, artfully used, with some responsive depth of his being that assimilates and is fashioned by them. Only thus can he attain that unselfconscious mastery of language that is known as style. Reading also helps him to live vicariously the lives of others, to observe with understanding and compassion, to stock the dark waters of his subconscious with fingerling perceptions and embryo emotions that will feed upon one another and grow unsuspected to their diverse maturities, ready to strike avidly some day when the bait is right and the angler diligent, or lucky. But to suggest that writers need to study others' writing in the sense and in the spirit that diplomats study world affairs, in order that they may decide what they should do and the manner of their doing it, this to me is ridiculous. What is important is not the extent of a writer's knowledge, but the use he makes of what he has.

Reading, however, is but a small part of most persons' total experience. Perhaps it will clarify the problem to ask whether those that lead the most varied and adventurous lives are of necessity the best writers. It is very evident that this is not true, if one may call such a motley as Goethe, Lamb and Balzac to witness. All the Bronte sisters line up alongside Thoreau to cock a comely snook at Durrell. Experience shapes the person, and the person writes; but it is the depth rather than the extent of the experience that will determine the significance of what is written, the degree to which it has been assimilated, made part of the writer's own blood and bone and emotional marrow. The writer that goes consciously in search of experience, subjecting himself to life in cold blood for the sake of "realism" in the work in which he is currently engaged, will seldom produce anything more than competent reporting. If such a writer produces a great novel, it is almost certainly in spite of his diligence in fact-gathering, not because of it. On the other hand, the writer that exposes himself freely to life in the conviction that in some way, at some time, his experience will be subtly and spontaneously transmuted into literature, that his random perceptions will be at the service of his pen when needed — not worrying himself too much about how it happens, or when — such a one, at last, refines the pure gold of his living.

In our lunch-hour discussion I made the rash observation that what is said is less important than how it is said. This of course brought howls of derision, but nevertheless in terms of literature it is true. Books survive the ravages of time and human fickleness not because they contain information, but because the manner in which their information is presented makes them literature. Truth somehow becomes more true for being well expressed. You can utter the most profound truths in the wrong words and convince no one, interest no one: but once pass the most mundane fact of life through the poetic process and it will uplift the hearts of the generations.

We are often told that writers reflect their own times and shape the thought of those that follow, and this is very true; but these are two very different functions, and the writer will fail if he is too self-consciously aware of either. It is great mistake to attempt to apply too directly his immediate experience if he aims at more than topicality. Everything he does will be coloured by his experience, by what he knows, but experience does not become significant until it has undergone the unpredictable alchemy of the creative process. Each writer finds he has a range in which he can work with true creativity. The result may bear little apparent relation to his own experiences. Often he finds that the aspects of his life that seem to offer the most promising and obvious material for his pen are in fact difficult or impossible to handle. If he tries, against his intuition, to impose his knowledge and experience upon his work, he will doubtless produce something informative, useful, wise and ephemeral. By submitting to the deep promptings of his assimilated life and learning, he may well, perhaps to his own great surprise, bring forth a *Kubla Khan* or an *Alice in Wonderland*.

No, it is not necessary to travel much, to experience much, even to read much in order to write books of timeless appeal: all that is needful is that the life that falls to the writer's lot be lived with a writer's perception, assimilated to himself, and wrought upon in the moment of creation in whatever manner his genius dictates.

The Birth of Words

Even in those dark days before "Up rose the sonne, and up rose Emelie" our literature was forming. While our fathers were clad yet in rudest garb and fought with weapons most primitive, the spirit of poetry moved them. Moved them not to odes and elegies but to the utterance of words. It elevated their intercourse from grunts and groans to cadences.

We spendthrifts of words concede them little thought, and less thanks, whose legacy we daily steal, and daily shame. Beautiful words abound, their creators forgotten but their fitness and authority still unchallenged. Those creators of common words were artists of a high order, but they are forgotten none the less.

He did not err, who named the moon. His life's essence, his immortality are in that word. It is his shrine. But it is a shrine at which none worship. We accept the word as if it grew out of the thing itself; as of course it did — that is the wonder and the beauty of it. It seems to have condensed and fallen perfect from the self-same gust of vapours in the silent womb of space, to have been polished to the moon's own lustre by the lips of the generations.

I like to think of that primitive Keats, standing at the edge of his world, at the shore of a sea teeming with mysteries, upon which no ship had ever been, the swathe of light lying softly upon the water like the touch of a woman, linking that glowing disc by a long bright thread to the very centre of his soul. He saw it perhaps as a knothole in the vast hollow tree of the universe, looking out upon a place where all was brightness and joy.

I can feel the word struggling to be born in him, swelling and shaping and ascending like a bubble in the muddy waters of his consciousness and springing at last from his lips with all the triumphant certitude of Archimedes' "Eureka!" And he listening to it there new and strange upon the night air as Handel, enraptured, must have listened to the first faint inklings of his Largo.

Fanciful indeed! But how fresh and meaningful our common words become when we think, however fancifully, of their beginnings. And how rich and sonorous in their simplicity those early words, that were born to satisfy not the demands of an expanding science but a hunger in the human soul; a hunger to share the burden of knowledge and wonder and speculation that one small head could no longer contain; to compare and so soothe the fears and superstitions of the long unsheltered nights, and to learn laughter at the good things of life, knowing the joy of them common among all people.

How different these words from the polysyllabic monstrosities we coin today: the words created by science with admirable system but without ear or imagination, and with a criminal disregard for the future of the language; the jargon spawned by specialists who are too preoccupied or too lazy to say what they mean; and the words invented by the ignorant to be foisted by commerce upon the public, or by a careless public upon itself. How few of these words go truly to the heart of things, take their meaning by the throat and ring out like the thing itself made sound. One shudders to think what modern man would find to call a tree, by what emotion-destroying horror from the lexicon of psychology he would define the elusive miracle of human love, or what dead epithet the gatherers of government revenue would attach to beauty, did they ever decide to tax it.

In the earliest days, the language was in the safekeeping of the poets; and since they strove always towards beauty of expression and language was proof against adulteration, words that were not easy on the ear died soon. Beautiful words for the beautiful, ugly words for the ugly: it should be law. Man at his most primitive knew as much. A rose by any other name would smell as sweet, but how grievously would the rose be wronged!

The worth of a word lies in its efficacy, in its evocative power. It is a wand to summon up like genies the elusive and otherwise impotent forces of meaning, by which alone misunderstanding can be vanquished, prejudice put to flight, the dark hordes of untruth routed.

Most of the words we invent today evoke nothing. They make cold appeal to the intellect but strike no spark from the imagination, no quick response from the emotions. They are not, like those words of old, spells to bring their objects magically to mind. We invent long unlovely words and then abbreviate them to our use. We pile prefix upon prefix, suffix upon suffix until we arrive at a word approximating the meaning of the word we started with, and fly to the dictionary to find what it is all about. True meaning was never found in a dictionary. It is only to be found by the lightning leap from mind to mind of a word that knows its job.

Specialists will tell you that these bastard words are necessary to precision. They lie. They conceive an elusive idea, or an abstruse one (ideas are only abstruse when ill-expressed), and to convey it succinctly they invent a word. This word they must then at great length define, thus debarring all who have not the leisure or the narrowness of scope to share their obsession. A word that needs definition is no word. There are few thoughts accessible to man's small mind that cannot be clothed in the language we already have. Not once in a decade does a writer, whether he write love lyrics or specifications for nuclear reactors, need to invent a word. When he does, never need it be clumsy, obscure, or an abomination in the ear.

Perhaps in addition to laziness, there is an element of cowardice in this retreat into the obscurity of new and turgid words. If I create a new word, perhaps the reasoning goes, who can gainsay me? I alone am master of its meaning. Philosophers have always been prone to this dereliction of their duty to be lucid. Psychologists have compounded the sin. Now semanticists, who should be very paragons of lucidity and good sense, are at it.

H. R. PERCY

One lesson a good writer learns slowly and with labour, and a bad one never, is that command of words is merely discipline of thought.